Josh Niland is the chef/owner of Saint Peter, a fish restaurant that opened in Sydney to widespread critical acclaim in 2016 and was shortlisted in the 2019 World Restaurant Awards Ethical Thinking category. In doing so, Niland started a conversation around boundary-pushing seafood, as well as winning every significant award in Australia for his world-leading approach to using the whole fish and wasting nothing. In 2018, Josh opened The Fish Butchery – Australia's first sustainable fishmonger – which sells dry-aged, cured and smoked fish and offal to an eager public as well as supplying a number of Sydney's best restaurants. *The Whole Fish Cookbook* is his first book.

THE WHOLE FISH
COOKBOOK

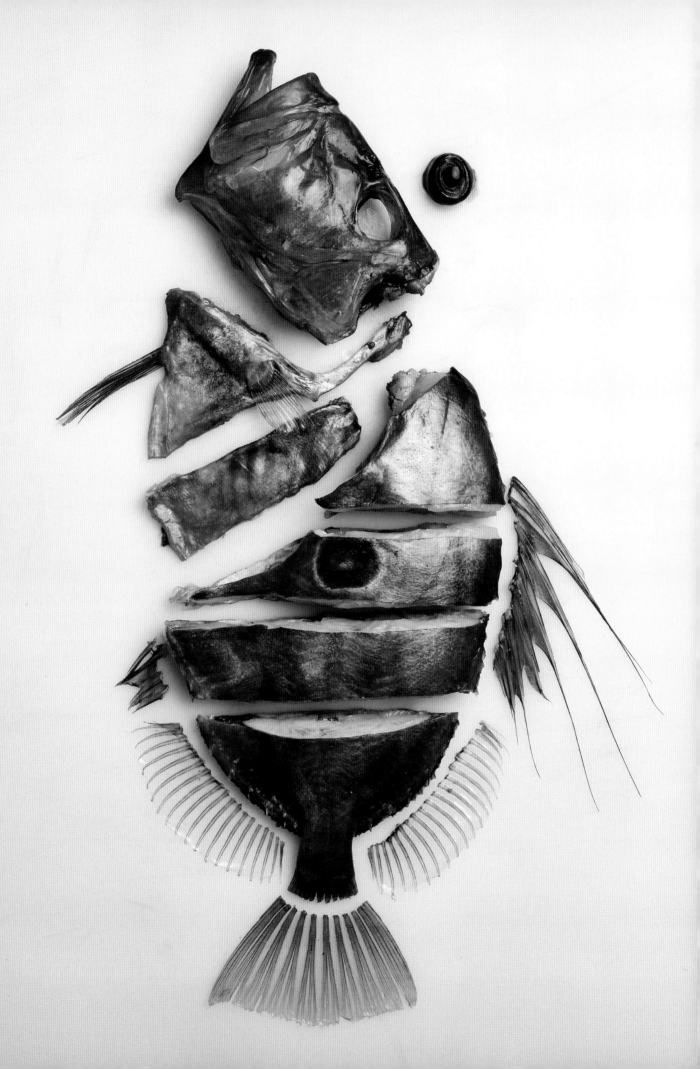

THE WHOLE FISH
COOKBOOK

New ways to cook,
eat and think

Josh Niland

Photography by Rob Palmer

Hardie Grant

BOOKS

CONTENTS

FOREWORD

Josh Niland is going to change fish for you forever. How you cook it, how (and how often) you eat it. It doesn't matter if you cook for a living or just for your friends and family. There's inspiration here for every skill level, from the tentative admirer of the firm white fillet to the professional gastronaut looking to set herself a challenge.

In Josh we find a chef not yet even at the height of his powers, driven to understand his subject almost literally at a cellular level, and working hard to answer the questions he uncovers along the way.

Why don't we cook more seafood at home? Does it always need so much acidity paired with it? Can we prep it without getting it wet? What happens when we age it more? Cook it less? And - most crucially for Josh, perhaps - why can't we use more of the fishes in the sea, and why can't we make more of each and every fish we buy? How can we do this better?

Nose-to-tail cooking of animals is readily accepted worldwide. The great British chef Fergus Henderson has made a life's work of celebrating cuts of meat, innards, and extremities that are more often forgotten or discarded in today's kitchen. 'It would seem disingenuous to the animal not to make the most of the whole beast,' he is fond of saying. Josh has set his mind to no less lofty a goal than bringing the same understanding and appreciation to the creatures of the deep. Send me whatever's in the best condition, he tells his suppliers, and I'll figure out a way to put in on the plate. That's what restaurant cooking is all about, isn't it?

That's the other thing. All the preparation and training in the world only means so much if you don't have inspiration. And Josh has that in spades. He is driven by muses prosaic and poetic – the fragrance of native parsley, the richness of the flavour of a kingfish after its fourth day in the coolroom, the neat way a boiled egg fits into the head of a small octopus.

His chief weapons in this mission are the taste and technique needed to make things powerfully appealing to the eye and the palate. He polished these skills at restaurants such as Glass, Est and, most notably, under the great seafood chef Steve Hodges at Fish Face in Sydney, as well as in the development kitchen at Heston Blumenthal's Fat Duck, but the things he has put on the plate at Saint Peter, the restaurant he opened in Sydney in 2016, are entirely his own. His Fish Butchery, a gleaming, fish-focused hybrid of an Apple store and a Damien Hirst installation, opened in Sydney in 2018 with the aim of nothing less than changing the very nature of seafood retail, and has been busy ever since.

Blood, guts and bones. You don't have to cook these things, but if you want to, Josh will show you how. (He also has smart ideas about what to do with mullet scales, trout throats and mackerel sperm, should you want them.) He'll also show you how to pick a fresh fish, poach it or crisp its skin. The only thing that excites Josh Niland more than exploring his subject is the chance to equip others with that same knowledge.

Plenty of other cookbooks hand the reader recipes. Josh wants to share with you what he has learned about the art and poetry of cooking itself. Give a person a fish, they'll eat for a day; teach them how to fish, they'll eat for a lifetime.

— Pat Nourse

INTRODUCTION

I am endlessly fascinated by the creative opportunities presented by fish. I love to work with fish because of its untapped potential, while its flavour, texture and appearance continue to inspire me to think more broadly about how to make it as desirable as possible.

Though I have been fortunate to work with some of the best chefs in the world (and have also had the pleasure of cooking with some of the globe's best produce), there are few better moments for me than when a customer comes up to the counter at Saint Peter, or the register at Fish Butchery, and enthusiastically conveys the positive fish experience they've just had. In opening these spaces, my wife, Julie, and I wanted somewhere we could celebrate not only the very best of Australian fish cookery but also demonstrate that there is *so much more* to a fish than the fillet and that there are far more than just a dozen fish in the sea.

This book takes that message to a wider audience. It is not just another seafood recipe book. You won't see any of the typical 'glamorous' images of fish sitting glistening on beds of freshly shaved ice here. Instead, I hope, you'll find a sense of dryness and approachability to the idea that fish isn't the smelly, slimy and bony ingredient that strikes fear into all of us, but is rather something that is individual – species to species and piece to piece – each coming with its own characteristics and a method of cookery that suits it best.

Around the time I started cooking fifteen years ago, there was a real respect growing around secondary cuts of meat. Looking back through notebooks, illustrations and cookbooks from that time, I can remember thinking how cool it was to be able to put half a dozen different parts of a pig, rabbit or cow on one plate and make it look desirable, luxurious and satisfying. On the other side of the coin though, fish has always been perceived as a more feminine, elegant and expensive ingredient that offers little potential beyond the fillet.

The knowledge I acquired working with meat proteins from a young age is now a hugely inspirational part of what I do with fish. To be able to work with the whole fish and put dishes together that feature both offal and fillet on the plate is thrilling for me – as less gets thrown away – but it's also exciting for our customers as they are able to see the luxury that lies within these ingredients.

Our entire way of thinking about how we process fish needs to be overhauled, with far more consideration given to the elements of a fish that would traditionally be considered 'waste'. Is this possible? Well, a lot of the most highly desired and most loved dishes in the world have been born from the utilisation of waste. Whether it is a terrine, sausages or the humble bread and butter pudding, all these dishes were born from that thought, 'What are we going to do with all this?' I don't see why fish should be any different.

Understanding the different parts of a fish and the methods of fish cookery thoroughly will put you in a better place as a cook to harness the potential excellence of every fish. A lot of what I want to offer throughout this book, then, is not so much the idea of why a fish should be paired with a specific garnish, but more about how to understand a fish better. Although cooking fillets may make up 45 per cent of this book, it's the other 55 per cent that's the most exhilarating. The latter is an invitation to explore fish more deeply and at the same time, learn to treat food more sustainably.

HOW TO USE THIS BOOK

My philosophy with fish is to minimise waste and maximise flavour. The two key tools that I use to achieve this are **whole fish cookery** and **dry-ageing**.

- Buying and cooking only fish fillets is not only creatively limiting but also neglects the majority of the fish – a shame, both from an ethical and sustainable point of view. Using the whole fish shows a great amount of respect for what is a globally depleting commodity.

- Dry-ageing (see page 29) enables me to enhance the unique flavour profile and texture of fish species in addition to allowing fish to be maintained in premium condition for longer. My knowledge of fish dry-ageing has been largely developed through trial and error.

The first half of this book details these tools in a way that provides new insights for domestic and commercial cooks alike, while the second half builds on them with recipes and ideas for further creativity. The fish featured in the second half of this book are by no means the definitive fish that must be used to achieve the same result – rather, they are a compilation of a few of my favourites and alongside that, there are alternative species suggestions for both Pacific and Atlantic waters. The key to good fish cookery is, above all, confidence and understanding of the species you are cooking, and the method you choose to apply to get the best possible result.

I hope this book both inspires you to select from a more diverse array of fish species and complementary methods of preparation, while also giving you a better understanding of an exciting new area of fish cookery.

THE KNO

WLEDGE

WHY *NOT* FISH?

I firmly believe that fish is the one protein that most of us would like to consume more of, as we are so aware of its valuable health benefits. So why, then, do we cook so little of it in our own homes in comparison to meat? Why *not* fish?

The following pages go into detail on the various different factors at play but first things first, let's address the thing that puts most people off entirely – cooking fish can be extremely difficult due to the exhausting number of variables involved. These range from what time of year it is, what hour of the day the fish was caught and how it was caught, to how it was then transported to market (or, in our case, direct to the restaurant) and the time frame in which this takes place. There's also the question of how the fish has been stored and prepared. Has it come into contact with ice or water after death? How has it been scaled? Has it been gutted? And how should it be cut? And that's all before you've got to the question of how, exactly, should the fish be cooked?

Seeing these variables written down looks overwhelming and some of these things might seem ridiculous or (to a degree) a little OCD, but for me, if one of these is not considered, the chain comes apart and the excellence in fish cookery that I want to achieve will not be possible.

To achieve best practice for all of these variables is no mean feat and is something that is probably not achievable on a mass scale. It is, however, what we strive to do at Fish Butchery and Saint Peter and what gives us, I believe, our point of difference. An understanding of these things, along with the rest of the factors at play that are detailed over the coming pages, will make a big difference to the way that you cook fish at home, too.

1. We lack a knowledge of fish or an understanding of fish cookery (or both!).

A negative experience with a fish will nearly always result in us either returning to what we are comfortable with or never attempting to eat or cook that fish again. The more I interact with customers at Saint Peter and (in particular) Fish Butchery, the more I've come to understand that buying raw fish for taking home to cook is broadly feared or put into the 'too hard' basket.

To have a positive experience cooking a raw fillet or whole fish we must talk with the person actually selling us the fish (see Sourcing, page 23) – or at the very least jump on our all-knowing smartphones – so that we have a basic understanding that goes beyond thinking we just need to pan-fry everything for the best results.

We all know that fish is a relatively expensive commodity that needs closer attention when cooking and handling than a boneless chicken thigh. But if it is a boneless fish fillet that you desire, then have a chat and see if this can be done for you. In a digital world where we are less and less connected to the food we eat, it needs to be said that you can (and should) talk with those people preparing and handling your food.

Buying a whole fish to take home, then scaling, gutting and filleting it may be far too laborious and time-consuming for your household, but remember that you can ask an attendant in a fish shop what is best or what they would recommend if they were to pick something. Alternatively, work out in your head what the main deterrents around fish are for you before buying and discuss these with the staff selling it to you.

Remember that our poor experiences with fish and our reluctance to diversify the fish on our table may not be because of the quality of fish we are buying but, instead, due to the application of cookery that we are choosing for that particular species.

While not everyone has an innate ability to touch, squeeze, smell and see when a fish is perfectly cooked, there are plenty of solutions – it might be as simple as switching to a better method of cookery that comes with a set time and temperature to remove the hurdle or confrontation that you feel about fish. In this book, I describe the many cookery methods that can be applied to fish, giving suggestions for a variety of different species as well as specific advice on what to look for when cooking a fish in a certain way in order to get the best out of it.

---

2. Good-quality, locally caught fish is both hard to come by and expensive.

Fish should not be looked at as an unchanging and always available commodity. It is rarely treated as a seasonal ingredient, which is a shame as there are so many moments through the year that provide extraordinary flavours and textures with fish. Yes, you can buy asparagus all year-round, but it will never be as close to perfection as the spears that land in the kitchen at the beginning of spring. Nor will the intoxicating floral aroma of a first-of-the-season peach be present in one eaten in the depth of winter from another country's summer. In much the same way, mirror dory in the cooler Australian winter months are excellent, but this fish is somewhat overlooked at times for its more glamorous relative, john dory.

John dory has a great texture when handled well, however, mirror dory can often be a little softer when it's not at its best and also somewhat challenging at times to cook given the depth of the fillet is so thin. At no other time throughout the year are the mirror dory quite as good as they

Other fish in the sea

A bad or negative experience cooking or eating certain fish can result in a lot of us forgoing branching out to other species. Salmon is a favourite table fish and is one of the most readily available fish in most shops. Skinless, boneless, nutritious and carrying more fats than most wild-caught fish, it provides a higher moisture content that makes it far less intimidating to handle than leaner fish such as mackerel, trevally (or mullet) and even flathead or bream, all of which can be more prone to drying out in cooking.

Salmon is seen by most as being a blank canvas, needing not to wow us with its nuances of flavour but, instead, being versatile enough to carry marinades, sauces and tolerate most domestic cooking applications. Although a lot of other species of fish come in at a lesser price than salmon at times throughout the year, it is still heavily sought after because the price and quality rarely fluctuate, and it is available every day of the year.

are in winter. The fish are firmer, they have a generous layer of fat that sits underneath the skin, the depth of the fillet is far thicker as the fish seem to be better nourished than they are if caught during warmer times of the year, and the offal of the fish can make up to 20 per cent of the fish's total weight.

A fish at its very best (height of its season) allows you to serve it confidently and proudly as a standalone dish and also gives you the opportunity to put every part of the fish together on one plate, meaning LESS WASTE. Starting to think about fish seasonally in the same way gives the cook the opportunity to serve it at its peak moment and get the most out of it.

Then there's the question of price. The average Joe can't just go and catch a cow for dinner, but he *can* catch a fish. So why should he be paying a lot of money? Well, the cost of that fish represents the same exhausting labour to the fisherman that a farmer of an animal would experience. The fragility of fish also plays a part in the cost; once that fish comes out of the water the clock starts ticking and a premium price for the highest quality can only be acquired by excellent handling from all involved.

The name of fish species can also determine the price tag or perceived value. There are more than a hundred different species of snapper worldwide, yet only a handful are the most trafficked and sought after based on consumer acceptance of the name of the fish. For example, a nannygai (closely related to the red snapper), which at the right time of year can be far cheaper than common snapper, will be the last to sell from Fish Butchery, regardless of it being line-caught, brain-spiked and packed as if it was a child's first Christmas present. The fact is that if this was placed on the display and labelled as a native Australian red snapper it would be more desirable.

In the second half of this book, I give suggestions for cooking a number of undervalued and less celebrated species, and have given details of alternative fish species in case the highlighted fish is either seasonally unavailable or is difficult to source in nearby waters.

---

3. Fish has a short domestic shelf life.

The short domestic shelf life of fish is often seen as a stumbling block in our efforts to cook and eat more of it, with spoilage rapidly apparent (see page 78 for details of 'fishy' fish). It is, however, a problem that is caused, primarily, by our means of production and storage.

A lot of the fish we buy from supermarkets and fish retailers – whether filleted or whole – has been heavily washed under running water in production, stored for a number of days and passed through a number of hands. It is also often then wrapped in plastic, then paper, vacuum-sealed or placed in plastic containers with plastic film set over the top, ready for us to transfer to the refrigerator for cooking and eating later.

Given that it has been washed under running water, this 'wet fish' retains a percentage of that moisture and, during this time of being left in the packaging, condensation forms on the inside of the storage container. This moisture promotes bacteria growth and often what we think is the right thing to do – which is to wash a fish thoroughly to remove any blood or debris – only helps contribute towards this major cause of a fish's short shelf life.

Thankfully, the dry handling of fish throughout the commercial process (see page 27), coupled with similarly good preparation and storage practice at home (see page 33) can do a lot to overcome this problem of excess moisture. I strongly encourage you to become familiar with the principles behind this, as they will make a huge difference to your understanding – and mastery – of fish cookery.

Equipment

Does a lack of equipment put you off attempting to cook fish at home? You don't need an elite kitchen full of fancy gadgets to produce excellent results with fish. The kitchen at Saint Peter could be best described as straight to the point, meaning we are limited by the space we have and also the amount of 'kit' we have to play with. We have eight thin black pans, six small and two medium saucepans, a double-pot deep-fryer, a single target top stove, one induction, two Japanese Konro barbecues and a professional oven for cooking our tarts each service. That's pretty much it. The list below is what I consider to be the essentials for fish cookery, but don't forget the most important rule: invest in the fish that you are purchasing and the results, as simple as they may be, will be superior.

Equipment Essentials

- Cast-iron frying pans
- Saucepan with a fitted lid
- Boning pliers and tweezers
- Fish weight (see page 135)
- Non-flexible sharp knives of varying lengths
- Chopping board
- Long tweezers (thin tongs)
- Offset palette knife

Once these principles of moisture removal are understood, this can be taken to the next level – experimenting with dry-ageing fish (see page 29) in a controlled environment to enable you to heighten or promote certain nuances in a fish's flavour profile.

4.   We don't necessarily know what good fish tastes like.

To be honest, having grown up in Maitland, NSW, Australia my first interactions with fish came in the form of tinned tuna and asparagus melts that my mum would have on her lunchbreak, the chilli oil-drenched tinned salmon that was decanted over salad leaves for a dinner from the pantry, and the fancy white anchovies from the tin that would be included on a Caesar salad at the local cafe. Little did I know at that point that tuna actually had a deep red flesh and little to no aroma, while salmon had orange flesh and those 'fancy' white anchovies started life as a fresh fish before being pickled with vinegar.

Call it a lack of culinary exposure as a child but, for most, this is normal – a lot of us go blindly through our younger years without having any basic understanding or appreciation for fish and seafood. It seems to be polarising – on one hand there are those who are spoilt by being exposed to a plethora of fish caught close to home or bought near a central fish market, and then at the other extreme, there are those who only know of tuna, salmon, anchovies and the occasional cooked king prawn (shrimp) at Christmas.

Similarly, when we're talking about eating fish, it's impossible not to factor in the issue of nostalgia. Take fish and chips, for example, which, along with being the most recognisable fish dish on the planet, is also the most difficult fish dish to execute consistently well. For our fish and chips there are about fifteen variables to achieve an excellent end result and only thirteen of these are controllable – the two that can't be controlled are in the customer's hands. The first, timing, can be taken into account to an extent (in 2019 a chef needs to consider how many potential photos a customer may take and upload to Instagram before beginning to eat). But the second – a customer's memory of a moment where they shared what may have been an average fish and chips with a loved one in the most perfect of locations, at the right time of day – cannot. For them, nothing will ever exceed that perfect fish and chips moment, no matter the effort that's invested in trying to cook it in a restaurant (or any other) setting.

To appreciate what good fish tastes like, it must start with adjusting the way you handle fish (see Fish Butchery Basics, page 39), then tasting the fish in its purest form, untouched by water. Eating fish raw (see pages 83–103) will help you understand the texture of fish to determine if it is soft or firm and if the flesh is fatty or lean. As well as eating raw fish, I find poaching fish (see pages 105–129) gives you an insight into what the flavour of the fish is really like. This, in turn, allows you to pick a suitable accompaniment for the fish that compliments, rather than complicates.

This isn't another fish book telling you to cook at home more, but one that is trying to help you make better decisions with fish, which, in turn, will give you better experiences with fish and will hopefully diversify the fish on your table, no matter where that table may be.

SOURCING

One of the most enjoyable parts of my day happens in the morning, when I have a text full of fish options from my buyer at the market. This interaction with him is crucial in making good choices for the restaurant and butchery. In addition to this relationship, we also deal directly with local and interstate fisherman. This allows us to work in slightly greater volumes and also eliminates some of the (understandable) middleman costs associated with going through market spaces.

Conversations with fishermen throughout the week are also important for giving our team at the restaurant an insight into their world as well as their struggles, whether those are weather-related or other unforeseen issues, as it helps us to understand the price value of the fish and why some fish just aren't available in a particular week. Direct rapport between the chef and the fishermen allows us to educate our front-of-house team not only about different fish species, but also about where a particular fish has come from. It is a powerful thing to be able to tell

a customer the name of the fisherman who caught their dinner.

Knowledge of the source of the fish can also inform us about its flavour profile. If you know that a fish has fed on crustaceans or seagrasses, then it can be slightly easier to recognise distinct flavours when tasting it. Understanding the flavour of a fish often aids in a better decision on what garnish to pair with it or even a logical method of cookery. Often, the flavour of a fish is described with adjectives, such as flaky, creamy or delicious, and not actual words that best highlight a potential flavour profile and which might encourage the consumer to diversify their choices. Too many fish have a bad rap for their perceived flavour profile and are thrown aside as inferior options.

Before any of this can be considered, though, we need to understand what it is we are actually looking for in regards to quality. Your instincts as a consumer should place you in the best position to buy an excellent fish, and the following details should all be taken into account.

1. **A fish with a firm mucus covering and shiny coating is the first sign of a good-quality fish.**

This is something you can check visually by looking at the scale coverage across the fish. The mucus of a fish was something that always seemed a mystery to me when I first started learning about fish. The mucus basically provides protection to the fish in the open ocean by trapping pathogens that would cause disease. Antibodies and enzymes in the mucus actively attack those pathogens to protect the fish. When an old mucus layer containing the pathogens is shed, it is replaced by new mucus and the pathogens are lost. Any visual damage or imperfections on a fish can suggest poor handling, prolonged direct ice contact or variable temperature control.

2. **The eyes of a fish are a determining factor of a healthy, fresh fish.**

A fish's eyes should look bulbous, be risen slightly from the head and look moist, bright and clear. There are, however, times when a fish that looks spectacular in every other way can have cloudy, slightly foggy eyes. This is predominantly due to the fish being chilled too quickly post-harvest.

Note: If you see a fish at the market with eyes that protrude considerably from the head, rest assured there is nothing wrong with it. This is an example of barotrauma, where a deep-sea fish has been caught at great depths and the large change in pressure caused by it being brought to the surface causes the eyes (and often also the stomach) to become more visually prominent than other species.

3. **A fresh fish should not smell fishy.**

As not every supplier or seller will allow you to handle the fish they are displaying, it is best to revert to your nose. Even the fish I dry-age for upwards of twenty days carry little to no aroma. The only smells a fish should have are a light ocean water smell sometimes comparable to mineral driven aromas, such as cucumber or parsley stems. If a fish smells 'fishy' (see page 78), with an odour comparable to that of ammonia or oxidised blood, then it is best to avoid it. Unfortunately, no matter how much culinary genius you may possess, there is very little that can be done to rectify a fishy fish.

4. **Iridescent bright red gills are an almost guaranteed indicator of the freshness of a fish.**

Fish force water through their gills, where it flows past lots of tiny blood vessels. Oxygen penetrates through the walls of those vessels into the blood, and, in turn, carbon dioxide is released. The redder the gills, the fresher the fish. Where slime and mucus are desirable on the outside of a fish, the gills should be slightly drier and clean of any debris.

The perception question: red mullet

A good example of skewed customer perception towards a fish is red mullet. Already in a consumer's eyes without talking to someone, a conclusion is drawn that it's mullet and must taste like the earthy, muddy and often 'fishy' fish that they may have grown up eating. Contrary to this, knowing that the diet of red mullet is rich in crustaceans will give us the knowledge that the fish also has a flavour profile reminiscent of lobster, crab or prawn (shrimp). A conversation when purchasing fish with the individuals handling or selling it will help guide you in the right direction.

The gills of a fresh, unaged bonito.

5. If your fish is frozen, look for freezer burn or crystals.

If you see them it means the fish has been thawed and refrozen, which affects quality. Overall, in terms of flavour and texture, fresh farm-raised fish is often preferable if a wild-caught product is unavailable and frozen is the only option. But if you decide to go with frozen fish, just know that some fish types do better in the freezer than others – lean white varieties, such as snapper and cod, tend to become dry when frozen, but the fattier types, such as tuna and Spanish mackerel, should be fine even when frozen.

This list of freshness quality points may, at first glance, seem hypocritical to the work we do at Fish Butchery and Saint Peter with regards to ageing fish (see page 29), but to produce profoundly unique flavour and texture profiles in aged fish, one must first find the most extraordinarily fresh fish and handle it well.

Finally, a word on sustainability. The topic of fish sustainability confuses home cooks and chefs alike. I see sustainability as a topic that requires a three-pronged approach. First, you need to be aware of the stock status of the fish species (this information is available online from your own local fisheries body). Second, you need to be aware of the practices of the fishermen who have caught your fish. Was the fish trawled in large nets or was it individually line caught? Finally, waste minimisation in the kitchen, which is achieved through both careful handling and storage of fish to maximise its shelf life as well as using the whole fish including its offal. This is explored further in the following pages.

Dry handling

If you purchase your fish whole, ask the assistant to scale and gut it without the use of water. If this is declined then it is best to scale and gut the fish yourself at home. It is a common assumption that gutting and scaling a fish at home will cause it to stink for weeks, but if handled correctly, the fish will smell less than one that has already been washed with tap water and wrapped in plastic for the car trip home.

STORAGE & DRY-AGEING

'Fresh is best' seems to be the most overused statement when it comes to fish. The truth is, the reason that most people enjoy eating fish straight off the back of a boat is because it pretty much tastes of nothing.

Very similar to a just-slaughtered cow, a freshly caught fish carries very little to no aroma or flavour. Dry-age that cow, however, and you enhance both its taste and consistency by reducing moisture and breaking down the enzymes within the animal protein. The same is true of dry-aged fish: though the desire here is not to break down any connective tissues as it is for meat but to reduce the level of unnecessary moisture present within the fish to heighten its flavour. Much like ageing beef, the ageing process for fish requires the same controlled environment where the temperature and humidity levels are carefully monitored.

The optimal storage conditions for fish are the same as for dry-ageing, which is why storage and dry-ageing go hand in hand – with dry-ageing you store select fish in these conditions for longer. Some fish are not suited to dry-ageing, but they will appreciate the same careful storage conditions as you would create for dry-ageing.

The steps to prepare fish for storage are the same whether you are receiving boxes of fish into a commercial environment or are bringing home a few fish from the market or shop.

First, source fish that hasn't been rinsed under tap water. Ideally, the last time your fish touched water was when it left the ocean. This will remain the case throughout the preparation of the fish. Fish is generally rinsed at market during the scaling and gutting process (a commercial necessity it seems, given the volumes). For this reason, I recommend scaling and gutting your own fish.

SCALING

Small fish, such as sand whiting, garfish and herring can be scaled with a small knife, small-headed fish scaler or spoon.

1. Gently run the scaler from the tail to the head working methodically around the body of the fish, applying only enough pressure to remove the scales. (To minimise mess from scales flicking off, you can work inside a clean garbage/bin bag.)

2. Continue until you are confident all the scales are removed, then wipe the fish and your chopping board with paper towel.

---

1. For large fish (plate size or larger) scales should be cut off if your knife skills allow for this. Starting at the tail end of the fish, hold your knife almost directly parallel to the bench while pressing against the scales and skin of the fish.

2. Angle your knife very slightly to allow the blade to slip between the scales and the skin, then, using a back and forth motion, begin to cut away the scales in long strips. The aim is to remove the scales while leaving the skin of the fish intact. The first few times you do this you may puncture the skin exposing the fish's flesh. Don't panic, simply correct your knife and continue. Keep the scales that are removed for other recipes (see page 69).

I recommend cutting off the scales like this from all large fish for several reasons. When scales are removed with a knife or fish scaler they are ripped from the 'pores' that hold them in position. This is problematic when the fish is rinsed as they soak up and store the tap water. Cutting off the scales preserves the skin so that it can be used as a barrier to protect the fish during storage. Fish prepared in this way is more suited to pan-frying on the skin, producing a crisp, crackling-like result.

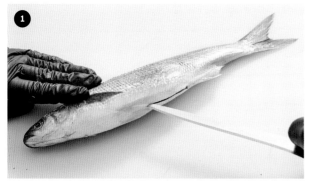

GUTTING

I believe that gutting a fish is only necessary if you are going to store the fish (as these will quickly turn the whole fish bad if left inside) or if you want to use the offal (which I do, of course, recommend). For those cooks experienced in fish filleting (see page 47), gutting the fish is unnecessary if you are going to fillet the fish straight away. Take care not to puncture the gut with your knife when removing the fillets. For those with less experience, gutting the fish prior to filleting may make the process easier.

1. To gut the fish, make an incision with a very sharp knife at the fish's anal vent. Using only the very tip of the knife, cut up through to the gills under the bottom jaw of the fish.

2. Once the cavity is opened, carefully separate the membrane that sits in front and behind the gills and the collar.

3. Spread the fish cavity fully open with both hands to expose the internal organs.

4. The gills can now be pulled down towards the tail, and all the internal organs of the fish can be removed in one piece with little mess. Done correctly, you should be able to hold the gills up above your board and the fish's offal will dangle below.

5. Wipe the cavity and skin of the fish very clean with paper towel. Reserve the offal (see pages 63–75).

Experimenting with dry-ageing

Ultimately, a perfectly aged piece of fish should still be succulent, juicy and offer 'fresh' qualities to the consumer. Fish such as Spanish mackerel, tuna and swordfish are excellent species to age for longer periods of time. They have a high fat content and dense muscle composition; two factors I have found favourable to lengthy dry-ageing. Fish with a slightly more open-textured profile, such as john dory, bream or flounder may only need four to five days to reach optimum flavour and texture. Other fish don't age quite so well, and in the case of delicate whiting, herring and slimy mackerel, for example, fresh sometimes is best. The reason behind this is that there is little fat in these fish and also minimal moisture content, so prolonged ageing would result in too much of this necessary moisture being lost.

Given the number of variables in play when ageing fish, try a piece of the fish each day to get a sense of how your refrigeration performs or how the particular species tolerates the conditions. Certain fish may reach multiple peaks of deliciousness over the period during which you age them and only by tasting them every day can you educate yourself about when these are. For more information on commercial dry-ageing, see the Appendix on page 247.

STORAGE

Scaled, gutted and untainted by water, your fish is now ready to store. Storage will vary depending on the size of the fish and your refrigerator. The key principles behind fish storage are:

- Low temperature, preferably between -2 and 2°C (28–36°F): fish deteriorates rapidly above these temperatures.

- Low humidity: it is important that the storage environment does not leave moisture on the fish's skin. Dry skin is essential to creating crisp skin when pan-frying.

- Prevention of 'sweating' from contact with surfaces: fish skin will sweat if left in contact with a surface for a lengthy period of time. Fish left sitting on a tray or plate will eventually create a pool of its own juices beneath it. These juices will speed up the deterioration process and create that 'fishy' smell. To prevent this, hang large fish from butcher's hooks in storage and store smaller fish and fillets on stainless-steel perforated trays.

- Prevention of drying out: fish left uncovered in a fan-powered refrigerator will quickly dry out and eventually become 'jerky'-like.

At home, I prefer to cook fish within two days of buying it. In this case it is sensible to fillet the fish (see Fish Butchery Basics, page 39) before storing, especially if fridge space is at a premium. What you want to avoid is the fillet drying out from the fridge fan, but also to prevent the fillet sitting in its own juices, which expedite deterioration. To prevent this, store your fillets, skin side up, on a wire rack placed in a tray or on a plate to catch the drips. Wire racks are usually not stainless steel so to prevent any reaction with the fish, perforate a piece of baking paper to separate the wire rack and the fillet. To prevent the fish drying out, store the fillets uncovered in the crisper. (If your crisper is filled with vegetables – as most are – loosely cover the fish with plastic wrap to prevent it drying out under the fan in the main chamber of the fridge.)

Regardless of your choice of crisper or plastic wrap, gently dry the skin just before cooking by placing the fish, unwrapped, in the main chamber of the refrigerator for 2 hours, or until the skin feels dry to the touch.

If storing fish for longer than two days, leave it on the bone. This reduces the chance of direct moisture contact on the flesh and minimises bacteria growth. First, select a fish that will fit whole in your refrigerator. Scale and gut the fish. It is best to cut the head off along with the collars to use immediately (see page 40), as these items do not age well in a domestic refrigerator with its frequent openings and fluctuating temperature. Keep the fish on a perforated tray and place in your vegetable crisper with the vents open. This way the fish stays at the lowest temperature and won't completely dry out. Each day remove the fish from the fridge and carefully wipe the surface with paper towel to remove any condensation on the skin or in the cavity. Alternatively, if the refrigerator you have is static and relies upon coil chilling rather than a fan, then you can use butcher's hooks or zip ties on the fridge racks to hang smaller species of fish.

Overleaf: Aged albacore; Day 20 (left), Day 3 (right).

FISH AS MEAT

Globally, meat is seen as a desirable protein. Whether it's grass or grain fed, we seem to have an inbuilt appreciation for it, we see the *value* in it – in the farmers who tend to their animals, in the butchers who age their cuts to a near perfect state of maturity and in the chefs who carefully roast and carve it. Meat butchery in particular, in recent years, has transformed itself into something glamorous that brings a sense of luxury to this relatively expensive ingredient.

The same cannot be said for fish. With a handful of exceptions, fish shops have remained relatively wet, cold and smelly places that are not overly pleasant to interact with. Yet there is no real reason that the two products should be treated so differently. After all, fish share with mammals the possession of a backbone (or vertebral column) and have fundamentally the same basic system of bones and organs as mammals.

Thinking about fish in the same way as meat is something that brings me a great deal of enjoyment and is what gave birth to Fish Butchery – a place that brings a touch of that glamorous vibe to fish and allows customers to interact with it in a different way. It's a place where you can request fish cut from the bone in a specific way to order, where fish has been aged to develop flavour and texture, and where you can interact with staff in a way that gives greater insight into the fish's provenance and methods of cookery for best results.

This way of thinking about fish stems from the time I first started writing my own menus in a restaurant. Back then, there were occasions when a fish would come in that I had never handled before. I would cook it as best as I knew how and then determine what meat category I could slip it into – whether that be lamb, beef, pork, chicken, game or offal. By categorising fish in this way, my garnishes became more considered and my diversity of cookery methods broadened beyond pan-frying.

Thinking of fish as meat also enables us to tap into the endless resources that are available to us in regards to meat methods and preparations that heighten flavour and texture, including dry-ageing (page 29) and curing (page 57) – ongoing pursuits for excellence for us as there are an extraordinary number of variables involved. Offal charcuterie is also a realm of unexplored opportunity where, again, the ever-changing list of variables at times seem more difficult to conquer than the recipe itself.

Finally, to disconnect completely from the fact that we are handling fish and not meat would be foolish. There have been many times when testing meat-based methods with fish that I have have applied too much seasoning, or used too much heat, both of which would be tolerated by meat proteins but not by their delicate fish counterparts. The key is to use 'fish as meat' as a way of looking at things differently to unlock the potential excellence that lies within every fish.

Left: *Yellowfin tuna, aged 20 days.*

FISH BUTCHERY BASICS

Butcher (v.) *the work of slaughtering animals and preparing them for sale as meat*

Monger (n.) *denoting a dealer or trader in a specific commodity*

When Fish Butchery opened, it was met with confusion by those who failed to see past the sign and read into what it was I was trying to do with fish. For me it was simple, and a logical extension of my thinking of fish as meat – fish can be cut and manipulated to be presented in unique ways that often look more desirable than uniformly coloured, skinless, boneless fillets.

The word 'butchery' comes with connotations of blood, bones and meat. Linking this to fish helps to provoke new thinking – whether it's in the way we cut fish, how we dress and present fish in a retail environment, even how our fish dish comes together on a plate. Through this thinking, certain parts of a fish that I had always looked at in a particular way became new to me and more value was placed on these overlooked parts.

The head and collars collectively (see page 40), for example, make up a large percentage of a fish's composition. Grilling the head and collars of a fish has now become quite common in restaurant kitchens for the reason that it is delicious and it doesn't require a great deal of work, as the head can be left whole or split in half for ease of cooking over charcoal or in a chargrill pan. Serving it with the fillet of the same fish feels generous, and you get to experience a completely different texture and flavour from the same fish.

We approach our work at Fish Butchery and Saint Peter with the customer always in mind and how they will interact with the end product. Yes, we encourage everyone to try fish offal and to diversify the species they select. At the same time we try to remove as much of the inconvenience as we can from the fish as possible, whether that's removing pin bones from a fillet or offering to crumb a boneless and butterflied King George whiting.

Before starting to scale, gut and fillet your next fish, try to visualise all the potential opportunities a fish presents. All of them can be achieved from one fish, so follow along and see the new culinary anatomy of a fish.

Key equipment

When preparing a whole fish, it's most important to determine the best knife to use. The first thing to do is throw out any flexible knives you own and invest in good-quality strong knives that feel comfortable and are extremely sharp. If you find yourself using your body weight to muscle fillets off the bone of larger fish then it might be time to sharpen your blade. Blunt knives make it difficult and dangerous to prepare fish, not to mention it will most likely take you ten times longer!

For a fish upwards of 1 kg (2 lb 3 oz) I prefer cutting the scales (see page 30), as it removes any unnecessary surface moisture that may speed up the deterioration of the fish and creates the opportunity to dry the exposed skin of the fish, resulting in a greater chance of a crisper skin. This will take some practice as the idea is to get the blade of the knife between the skin and scales and, using a gentle sawing motion, make your way in strips from the tail to the head.

For gutting a fish, use a shorter blade to avoid the length of a blade puncturing the internal organs. Another useful tool in this process is a sharp pair of scissors; sometimes getting a knife through some of the hard bone and cartilage surrounding the gills can be challenging, especially on large fish.

HEAD BREAKDOWN

Coral trout head (aged 3 days).

1. Head
2. Throat
3. Cheek plate
4. Eye
5. Bottom jaw

6. Jowl
7. Collar
8. Top jaw
9. Cheek
10. Tongue

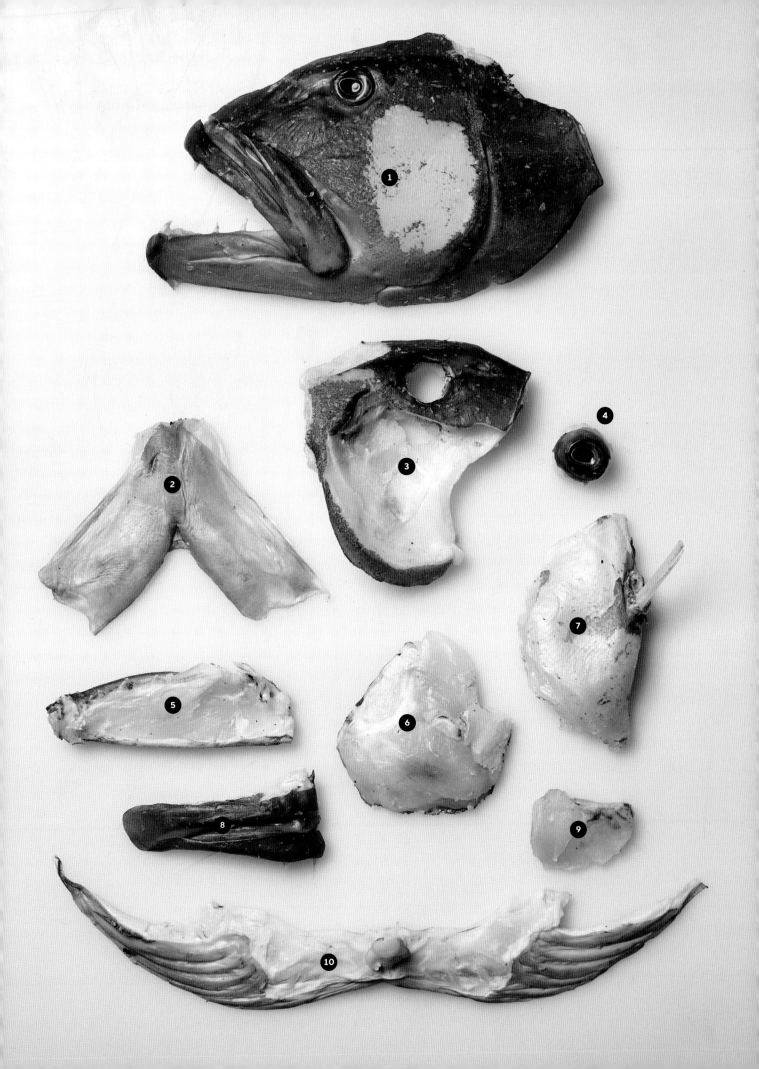

WHOLE FISH BREAKDOWN

Bass grouper (aged 2 days).

1. Scales
2. Top lip
3. Tongue
4. Top jaw
5. Bottom jaw
6. Eye
7. Cheek
8. Jowl
9. Bone-in jowl and cheek
10. Collar
11. Throat
12. Heart
13. Bone marrow
14. Blood
15. Liver
16. Spleen

17. Stomach
18. Belly
19. Forequarter rack
20. Mid-loin fillet

21. Spare ribs
22. Bone-in red muscle
23. Swim bladder
24. Top loin

25. Spiny dorsal
26. Soft dorsal
27. Mid loin
28. Hindquarter rack

29. Tail-end fillets
30. Anal fin
31. Skin

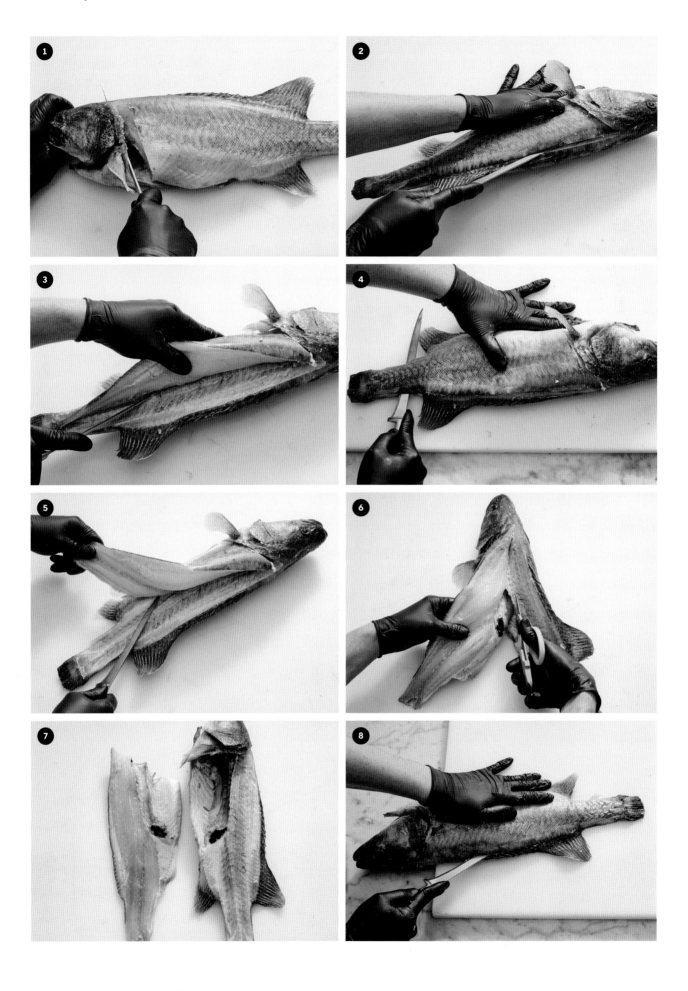

FILLETING

For the first cut, place the fish with the belly facing you and the head to the left (or the right if you are left-handed).

1. Pull the pectoral fin outwards and make a cut behind these fins to separate them from the fillet, then cut around behind the head until you hit bone. By doing this you are effectively separating the fish collars from the fillet.

2. Turn the fish so the belly is facing away from you, (head on the right, tail left) then, starting from the cut at the top of the head, cut along the backbone from the head to the tail, cutting smoothly along the length of the fillet.

3. Angling your knife towards the bones, keep running your knife along where the flesh meets the bones to open out the fillet until you feel your knife reach the raised spine in the middle. Using your knife, stay as close to the spine as possible and go over the bone.

4. Place the knife flat against the backbone and push the point through to the other side of the fillet. With the knife protruding out the other side and pressing against the spine, cut all the way to the tail to separate the tail section.

5. Turn the fish so the belly faces you and lift the tail section to expose the ribs.

6. Snip through the ribs with kitchen scissors up to the first cut.

7. You can now remove the first fillet.

8. Flip the fish so the belly faces away from you and the head points left. Hang the head off the edge of the board so the fish lies flat (this way you'll be able to cut evenly and preserve more flesh). Repeat the first cut, then cut along the back through the rib bones and, guiding the knife by pressing it against the ribs, cut towards the pin bones.

9. Turn the knife the other way and, using the bones as a guide, cut up and against the ribs, gently peeling away and slicing as you go.

10. Cut the second fillet away from the frame using scisssors and wipe clean with paper towel.

Note: The fish used here to demonstrate the filleting process is an aged Murray cod (aged 7 days).

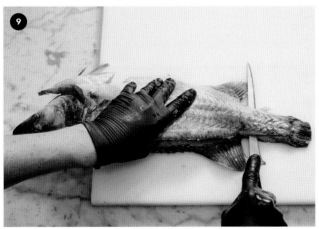

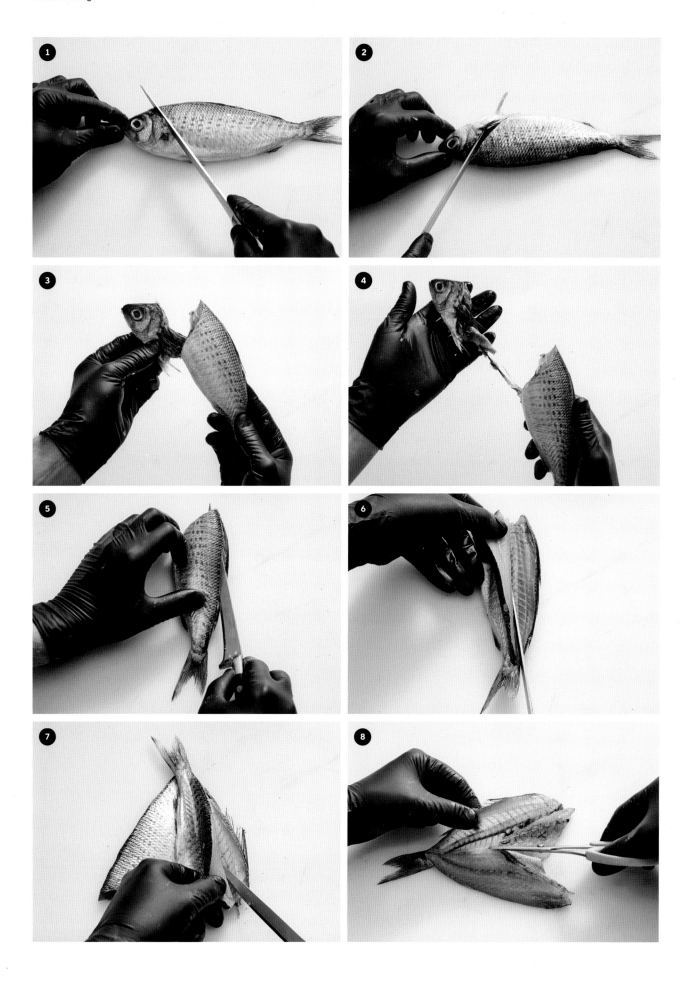

BUTTERFLY

Assuming you're right-handed (otherwise reverse these directions), place a fish on a chopping board with its head to your left and tail to your right.

1. Start by making a cut just behind the head on a diagonal that runs parallel to the fish's wing bones.

2. Flip the fish over and repeat the cut as before.

3. When these two cuts join up, pull the head of the fish off by gently breaking it off the spine.

4. As you pull the head, ensure that the fish's gut is pulled with it. If successfully done, this is a fast and clean way of gutting the fish. It's important that the gut is taken out like this, as we want to keep the belly intact.

5. Draw your knife down the backbone of the fish from the head end to the tail, cutting along one side of the bone.

6. Cut again to deepen the initial cut, carefully cutting all the way through (but not to puncture the belly) to open up the fish, leaving the tail intact.

7. Turn the fish around so the tail is facing away from you and repeat on the other side of the backbone.

8. Using kitchen scissors, snip out the backbone to give a kite-shaped fish with the tail intact. Use fish tweezers to remove pin bones and rib bones. (Alternatively, depending on species, it may be easier to remove the rib bones with a small, sharp knife.)

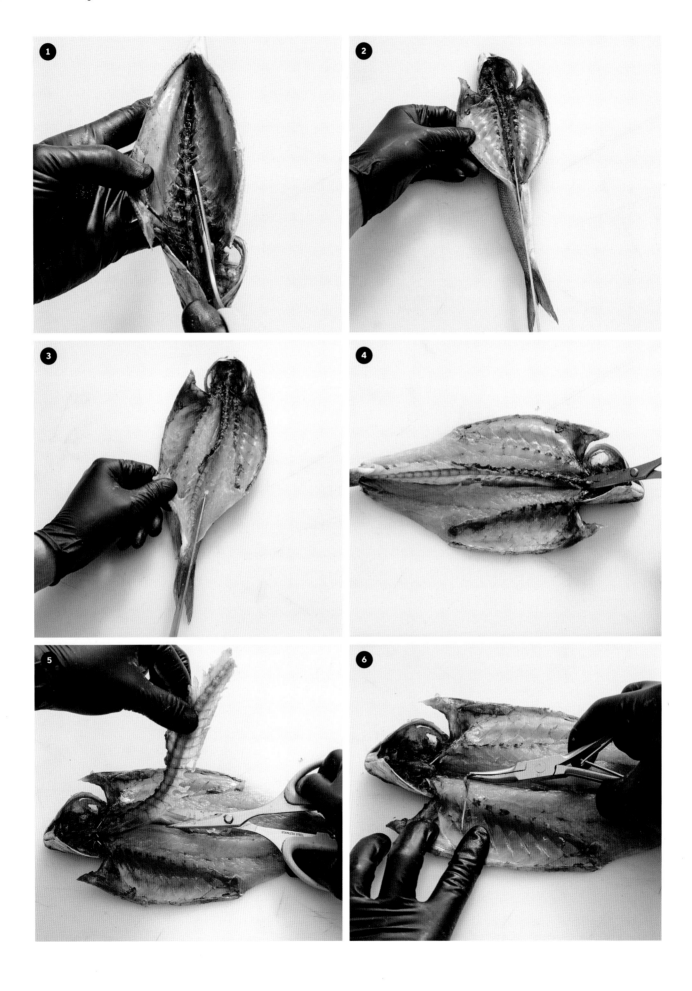

REVERSE BUTTERFLY

Make sure the fish is scaled and gutted conventionally before attempting this method. Position the fish in front of you with the head nearest to you and the tail furthest away.

1. Using sharp kitchen scissors, begin cutting down the left-hand side of the fish spine to disconnect the ribs from the spine, but stop at the fish's anus. Repeat this step down the right-hand side of the spine. This now gives you a clear track to use your knife in the next step.

2. Position the fish now with the head facing away from you. Using a small, sharp knife, draw the blade down the scissored opening that you have made next to the spine.

3. Repeat on the opposite side.

4. When these two cuts meet up at the tail, use kitchen scissors to snip the tail, then just behind the head where it meets with the spine.

5. Pull the spine carefully off the skin of the fish making sure to support the surrounding flesh so it doesn't rip or do damage.

6. Use fish tweezers to remove pin bones and rib bones. (Alternatively, depending on the species, it may be easier to remove the rib bones with a small, sharp knife.)

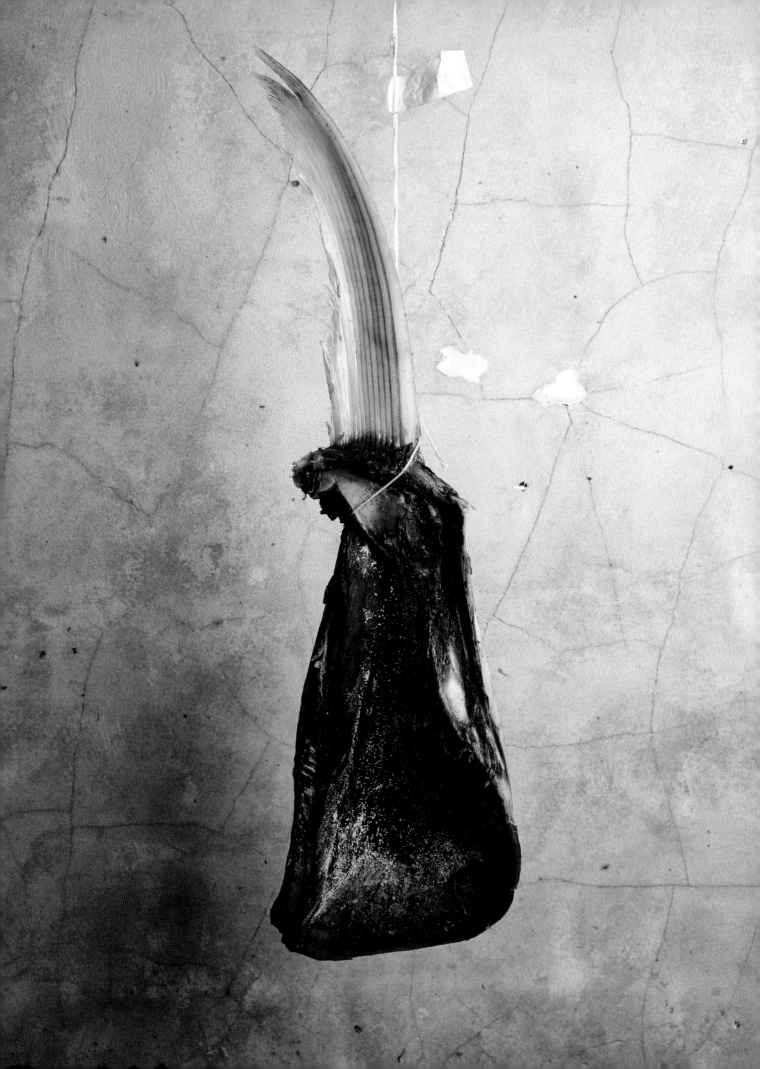

CURING

When dealing with a protein as delicate as fish that's prone to spoiling, it is important to understand the preservation methods that are needed in your culinary artillery to combat waste. The curing of fish has been seen for centuries as one such method of preservation – its primary function being to draw moisture out of food by the process of osmosis.

At Fish Butchery we use curing as a way to bring value to those less appreciated parts of the fish. Be it the hearts, spleen, thin belly flaps with little flesh, or those smaller fish that may be perfect to eat raw from days one to three but lose their lustre quickly. As we handle large volumes, we don't see the need to purchase fish with the single purpose to cure. Rather, we cut what we need for fresh and the cuts that don't present the way we want become cured or processed items.

I was fortunate when I opened Fish Butchery to employ the talents of Paul Farag. Paul had years of experience as a restaurant chef working in some of the best kitchens in both Sydney and London. The first day I spoke with him about working together at Fish Butchery, he was a little hesitant, as his previous experiences and training had been predominantly meat focused, but I felt this was in fact a huge advantage in terms of what I wanted to achieve.

Curing a fish that's in season and at its peak is a way of suspending a particular moment in time that will yield a far better result. Just remember that when handling raw and cured fish, it is imperative that the strictest of hygienic conditions are demonstrated. Wear disposable gloves to handle your fish at all times and be sure to use sterilised containers for storage.

Left: Moonfish guanciale.

Paul's Spiced Marlin Ham on the Bone

This extraordinary ham is one that Paul Farag developed very early on at Fish Butchery, and it showcases both his creativity and flawless technique. If you can't find striped marlin, use tuna, albacore, swordfish, spearfish or moonfish instead. For this particular recipe, I recommend you use the lower half of the fish. Request that the fish be cut just below the anus so that the flesh that remains on the bone is free of pin bones (the shape of this section of the fish also resembles a leg of ham).

MAKES 3.5 KG (7 LB 12 OZ)

3–4 kg (6 lb 10 oz–8 lb 13 oz) striped marlin tail

Brine
400 g (14 oz/1⅓ cups) fine salt
8 litres (260 fl oz/32 cups) cold water

Cure mix
10 g (¼ oz) fenugreek seeds
10 g (¼ oz) cumin seeds
20 g (¾ oz) yellow mustard seeds
20 g (¾ oz) ground turmeric
200 g (7 oz/⅔ cup) fine salt
70 g (2½ oz) caster (superfine) sugar
2 g (½ teaspoon) nitrate

To skin the fish, draw a small, sharp knife around the border of the fish, then working from right to left, coax the blade under the thick skin. Make small cuts to help peel the skin off the exterior of the tail.

For the brine, stir the salt and water together in a sterilised plastic container. Place the tail in the brine and leave for 3 days.

On the fourth day, toast the whole spices in a frying pan over a low heat for 1 minute, or until fragrant, then transfer to a spice grinder or mortar and pestle and grind to a powder.

Combine all the cure mix ingredients in a large bowl.

Remove the fish from the brine, pat dry and rub liberally with the cure mix, then place in a large, clean plastic container lined with baking paper. Place a fitted tray on top of the fish to weight it down and store for 2 weeks, turning the fish every day.

Once the fish is firm to the touch and has a uniform turmeric stain on the outside, use kitchen twine to tie the tail up and hang it in a fan-forced refrigerator to continue developing the flavour. Alternatively, a wire rack in a tray will achieve a similar result, as long as the ham is well ventilated. Leave for at least 4 weeks, but if you can't wait this long, then thinly slice the fish from the bone and serve as a cured fish.

To serve, slice from the bone and serve with chutney or on toast with plenty of black pepper and extra-virgin olive oil.

Curing at home

When curing at home, a simple curing ratio of 60 per cent salt and 40 per cent sugar can be used to suit a long list of fish species. Mix 1.2 kg (2 lb 10 oz) salt, 800 g (1 lb 12 oz/5⅓ cups) sugar, 1 tablespoon toasted fennel seeds and 1 tablespoon toasted coriander seeds together in a large bowl. Store in a clean mason (kilner) jar or plastic container. For the best results, use 200 g (7 oz) of the curing seasoning per 1 kg (2 lb 3 oz) boneless flesh. Rub the curing mix over the fish, then place on a clean deep-sided dinner plate. The juices that are extracted from the curing will produce a brine. Turn the fish over once a day for three days until the curing has firmed the flesh up completely, then set the fish on paper towel to dry slightly. Using the back of a knife, gently scrape off any surface juices from the fish, then slice thinly and eat. Alternatively, after draining, rub the fish with spices or other seasonings, such as herbs, aromatic spices or even ground coffee, to add another level of flavour. Assuming you have cured the fish with the skin on, you can also grill or pan-fry the fish (see pages 131–175).

Swordfish Bacon

This recipe for swordfish bacon relies so much upon the swordfish being of the highest quality. As when curing meat products, the greater the amount of fat, the greater the flavour. When at its best, swordfish has an extraordinary amount of intramuscular fat, lending itself so well to this style of preparation. The cure mix yields 140 g (5 oz) finished seasoning. We recommend using 120 g (4½ oz) cure mix per 1 kg (2 lb 3 oz) swordfish loin.

MAKES 800–900 G (1 LB 12 OZ–2 LB)

1 kg (2 lb 3 oz) A+ grade swordfish loin or belly, cut into 4 x 250 g (9 oz) prisms
2 x 14 g (½ oz) soaked hickory or cherry wood pucks

Cure mix

40 g (1½ oz) caster (superfine) sugar
80 g (2¾ oz/¼ cup) fine salt
1 star anise, lightly toasted and cracked
15 g (½ oz) thyme leaves
¼ teaspoon nitrate
1 tablespoon lightly toasted and cracked black pepper
1 fresh bay leaf, finely chopped

Combine all the cure mix ingredients together in a clean bowl. Rub the swordfish with the mix until it is completely covered, then place on a stainless-steel gastronome tray or clean plastic container lined with baking paper. Cover with baking paper and refrigerate. Leave for 7 days, turning the fish every day.

When the fish is cured, remove from the tray and pat dry with paper towel.

Cold smoke the fish in a smoker for 40–45 minutes depending on your desired degree of smokiness. Alternatively, line the top of a double steamer with foil, add soaked wood chips in the base and use this to cold smoke the fish.

Remove from the smoker and, using kitchen string, truss the fish, then hang on a hook in a fan-cooled refrigerator for 3–5 weeks to dry. Once ready, store on the hook or slice and store in an airtight plastic container.

The bacon can be finely sliced and eaten as a cold cured item, similar to smoked trout, or can be thickly cut into lardons and caramelised in a frying pan for a great addition to peas and lettuce. The sky's the limit!

Cured & Smoked Brown Trout

Brown trout is an excellent eating fish, and one that doesn't get enough attention. In this preparation, we cure it with light muscovado sugar and toasted coffee to impart a robust flavour. When served like this with good-quality rye bread, salted butter and celery, this overlooked fish is transformed into something that can happily sit beside the most premium of smoked salmon products.

MAKES 1 KG (2 LB 3 OZ)

1 kg (2 lb 3 oz) boneless brown trout fillets, skin on
1–2 x 14 g (½ oz) soaked apple wood pucks

Cure mix

½ teaspoon good-quality whole roasted coffee beans
55 g (2 oz/¼ cup) fine salt
40 g (1½ oz/¼ cup) dark brown sugar

Gently crack the coffee beans in a mortar and pestle. Don't grind the coffee into a powder as the flavour will be too dominant. Mix the cracked coffee with the salt and sugar well.

Rub the cure mix evenly over the fillets, including the skin, then place the fillets onto a stainless-steel gastronome tray or clean plastic container, flesh side down, cover with baking paper and refrigerate. Leave for 3 days, turning the fish every day.

Once the fish is firm to the touch and the dry seasoning is now a flavoursome brine, remove the fillets and, using a small palette knife, gently wipe away any residual brine.

Cold smoke the fish in a smoker for 30 minutes depending on your desired degree of smokiness. Alternatively, line the top of a double steamer with foil, add the soaked wood chips in the base and use to cold smoke the fish.

Remove from the smoker, place on a wire rack inside a stainless-steel gastronome tray or container and chill overnight, uncovered.

The next day, slice the trout thinly from the tail to the head and serve at room temperature with good rye bread, celery and salted butter.

Moonfish Guanciale

When we developed this recipe, we were fascinated to learn that moonfish is a warm-blooded species of fish. The meat that sits adjacent to the gills and around the head is extremely dark – a similar colour and texture to that of beef or venison. With an adjustment of some of the spices, this curing mix complements the dark meat of this unique fish. If moonfish is unavailable, this recipe will work with most tunas and mahi-mahi. Patience is required here for best-textured results.

MAKES 1.8–2 KG (4 LB–4 LB 6 OZ)

1 × 2 kg (4 lb 6 oz) dark flesh moonfish piece

Cure mix
80 g (2¾ oz/⅓ cup) caster (superfine) sugar
160 g (5½ oz/½ cup) fine salt
2 star anise, lightly toasted and cracked
30 g (1 oz) rosemary leaves, finely diced
½ teaspoon nitrate
2 tablespoons lightly toasted and cracked black pepper
1 tablespoon ground juniper
½ teaspoon freshly grated nutmeg
2 fresh bay leaves, finely chopped

Combine all the cure mix ingredients in a clean bowl, then rub the fish with the mix until it is completely covered. Place the fish on a stainless-steel gastronome tray or in a clean plastic container lined with baking paper, cover with baking paper and refrigerate. Leave for 7–10 days, turning the fish every day.

Once the fish is cured, remove from the tray and pat dry with paper towel.

Using kitchen string, truss the moonfish. Hang the fish on a hook in a fan-cooled refrigerator for 4–6 weeks to dry. Once ready, store on the hook or slice and store in an airtight plastic container.

A fantastic way to eat this guanciale is to pan-fry batons of this ham and use them in your next carbonara pasta.

Wild Kingfish Pastrami

Unlike most of the recipes in this section, this takes considerably less time to cure. Wild kingfish is one of my favourite fish, especially when treated like this. The use of lemon myrtle, fennel and coriander seeds highlight the fish's natural acidic qualities. Other fish that carry these same qualities are amberjack, samson, hamachi and yellowtail.

MAKES 1 KG (2 LB 3 OZ)

1 kg (2 lb 3 oz) boneless wild kingfish fillet, skin on

Cure mix
40 g (1½ oz) caster (superfine) sugar
80 g (2¾ oz/¼ cup) fine salt
1 tablespoon ground fennel seeds
¼ teaspoon nitrate
1 tablespoon ground coriander seeds
1 fresh bay leaf, finely chopped

Seasoning rub
2 tablespoons lemon myrtle
1 tablespoon freshly ground black pepper

Combine all the cure mix ingredients in a clean bowl, then rub the fish with the mix until it is completely covered. Place the fish on a stainless-steel gastronome tray or in a clean plastic container lined with baking paper, cover with baking paper and refrigerate. Leave for 3–4 days, turning the fish every day.

Once the fish is cured, remove from the tray and pat dry with paper towel.

Combine the seasoning rub ingredients. When ready to serve, season this mixture over the fish and slice the flesh straight off the skin from the tail to the head. Serve at room temperature.

FISH OFFAL

Fish isn't as cheap as it once was and there are fewer and fewer skilled hands processing it. So, driven by the pursuit of efficiency and the demand for quantity over quality, we seem to have pumped the brakes on investigating its potential and settled for what has always worked.

Such an approach is extremely wasteful.

As a chef, you are broadly educated that a round fish will yield anywhere between 40–45 per cent. I can't comprehend how this is acceptable globally? Surely, instead of reading countless recipes about the many methods of cookery and flavours that can be applied to the 40 per cent, we should shift our attention to the majority, which offers the greatest amount of culinary opportunity.

Fish hearts, spleens, blood and scales were all very foreign to me until I opened Saint Peter and started preparing them in similar ways to meat-based recipes. As chefs, we are familiar with meat offal and how to use it, so this was a useful technique to developing recipes for these parts too. Thinly sliced fish heart threaded onto a skewer and grilled over charcoal is a textural triumph for an organ that is susceptible to dryness and chewiness due to its low fat content,

while fish blood makes a delicious black pudding (blood sausage) with a cleaner flavour than most pigs black pudding.

It is interesting that in the three years the restaurant has been open, the desire to eat fish offal continues to grow. Call it a fad but while the audience is captive it is a great way to share the potential of how flavourful and nutritious fish organs can be. This can put pressure on us to have it always available on the menu, which unfortunately given the variable nature of fish isn't always possible. A fish has one heart, one liver, one spleen, a handful of scales and the potential of a roe sack or milt sack. If any of these items show any discolouration, imperfection or damage, they will not be used, regardless of the demand.

Attempting fish offal for the first time at home can feel intimidating. My best advice would be to start with something as basic as a fish liver on toast (see page 160). Next time you visit your local fish shop or market, ask what livers are looking good or in which season they will likely be at their best. The best approach to pan-frying a fish liver is to treat it as you would any chicken or duck liver, pink and warmed through with a tan crust on the outside.

Puffed Fish Skin

Puffing fish skin seems fairly common. At one point in the restaurant we were using quite a lot of ling, which has an extremely tough skin that has little chance of breaking down if left on the fish during cooking. As a result, we reserved all the skins from one day of processing, scraped away all the sinews and flesh that remained, and created this.

Once all your fish skins have been scraped, bring a saucepan of water and a pinch of salt to the boil over a high heat. Working with one skin at a time, blanch the skin for 20 seconds then remove it with a slotted spoon. At this point the skin is quite delicate and prone to puncturing or tearing so carefully spread it out flat on a baking tray lined with baking paper.

Once all the skins are evenly spread out, leave in an oven set to the lowest temperature held ajar with tongs, or use a dehydrator set to 85°C (185°F). Once they are completely dry, store in an airtight container or vacuum pack bag indefinitely for later use.

To puff the skins, heat a pan half full with grapeseed, canola (rapeseed) or cottonseed oil over a medium-high heat until it reaches 185–190°C (350–375°F) on a probe thermometer. Very carefully use a small set of tongs to add the dried skin to the oil and within 5–10 seconds the skin will triple in volume. Remove quickly so the skin doesn't colour as it will become bitter. Season liberally with salt and serve.

Offal basics

When selecting fish offal, ask for what has been only dry handled and not left in a bucket of blood-tainted water as this will be detrimental to the flavour. Visually the offal should look clean, bright and slightly moist. There should be little to no aroma and the organs should be firm to the touch and not discoloured, soft or slimy.

Fish offal, like most meat offal, should be consumed the day you purchase it. Freezing fish offal has mixed results. The hearts, stomach, spleen and blood all freeze well, but items like the liver, roe and milt depending on the usage tend to break down and become slightly mushy when thawed.

Eye Chip

This recipe represents the amazing effort of the extraordinarily talented team that I had in the kitchen in Saint Peter's first year. It was always the ambition to try to find a delicious use for every part of the fish. As a collective we considered that a prawn (shrimp) chip was merely blended prawn and tapioca starch transformed into a wonderfully crisp, light and flavourful chip. So, this thinking of a prawn chip led us to producing this fish eye chip. The eyes must be the freshest possible and be sure to wear disposable gloves at all times when making this.

MAKES 12 LARGE CHIPS

150 g (5½ oz) fresh fish eyes
100 g (3½ oz) calamari eyes
125 g (4½ oz/1 cup) tapioca flour
canola (rapeseed) or vegetable oil, for deep-frying
salt and freshly ground black pepper

Blend the fish and calamari eyes in a blender to produce a thin runny grey liquid, then pass this liquid through a very fine sieve until it's completely smooth. Using a rubber spatula, beat in the flour until it looks similar to the consistency of thick cream. Spread the batter out onto a sheet of baking paper cut to fit a bamboo steamer and steam over a pan of boiling water for 10 minutes.

Place on a wire rack and leave in an oven set to the lowest temperature held ajar with tongs or use a dehydrator set to 85°C (185°F) to dry into a chip.

When completely dry, half-fill a deep saucepan with oil and heat until it reaches 190°C (375°F) on a probe thermometer. Snap off a piece of the chip and deep-fry very quickly for 10 seconds until the chip doubles in size. The final result of the chip will look similar to a prawn cracker or pork crackling. Drain on paper towel and repeat with the rest of the chip.

Season and serve on its own or as a vehicle for raw fish or even sea urchin.

Puffed Fish Swim Bladder

Puffing the swim bladder follows the same method as puffing fish skin (see page 64), the main difference being that once the swim bladder is removed from the fish, the bladder is cut down one side then laid out flat in front of you.

Using a pastry scraper or knife, carefully scrape the bladder back and remove any imperfections or thickness to make it an even size during cooking. Unlike the short blanching time required for the skin, cover the bladder with cold water in a pan and add any desired aromatics, such as seaweed, thyme, tarragon, wine, etc. Bring the liquid to the boil then reduce the heat and barely simmer for up to 20 minutes until it softens completely. The time this takes depends on the swim bladder size and species type. (The object here is to tenderise and impart flavour to what is a very neutral tasting part of the fish.)

Carefully remove the bladder from the liquid then spread it out on a baking tray lined with baking paper. Place in an oven set to the lowest temperature held ajar with tongs, or use a dehydrator set to 85°C (185°F). Once the bladder is completely dry, store in an airtight container or vacuum-pack bag for later use.

To puff the swim bladder, heat a saucepan half full with grapeseed, canola (rapeseed) or cottonseed oil over a medium–high heat until it reaches 185–190°C (350–375°F) on a probe thermometer. Very carefully use a small set of tongs to add the dried bladder to the oil and within 5–10 seconds the bladder will triple in volume. Remove quickly so the bladder doesn't colour as it will become bitter easily. Season liberally with salt and serve.

Offal XO Sauce

Variations of XO sauce are forever coming in and out of fashion as they carry a great amount of umami and fantastic texture if cooked correctly. I have used salted chillies in this recipe to remove some of the intensity from the heat that an XO sauce sometimes has. Serve this sauce with fish, roast meats, vegetables and rice dishes. It stores well and only gets better with time if handled correctly and kept in an airtight container or sealed vacuum-pack bag.

MAKES 700 G (1 LB 9 OZ)

500 ml (17 fl oz/2 cup) grapeseed oil
150 g (5½ oz) spring onions (scallions), finely diced
150 g (5½ oz) finely diced fresh ginger
75 g (2¾ oz) finely diced garlic
250 g (9 oz) finely diced salted chilli (see note)
75 g (2¾ oz) each dried, smoked and finely diced fish heart, spleen and roe (see page 74)
75 g (2¾ oz) smoked and diced Swordfish Bacon (see page 60)
1 tablespoon freshly ground black pepper
1 tablespoon ground toasted fennel seeds

Heat the oil in a wide-based frying pan or large saucepan over a medium heat and wait until there is a light haze over the pan. Add the spring onions, ginger and garlic and cook for 10 minutes, stirring to avoid the ingredients catching or taking on too much colour. When the vegetables are lightly tanned, add the salted chilli, dried offal, bacon and spices and stir well to coat in the oil. Reduce the heat and cook for 30–45 minutes more to condense all the flavours. (Avoid seasoning with salt as the chillies aid in the seasoning of this sauce.)

Spoon the sauce over cooked vegetables, meats or fish. This is such a delicious and unique condiment to use for any occasion – even through scrambled eggs at breakfast!

Note: Salted chillies are chillies that have been split in half, seeds removed then buried in rock salt for 3–4 weeks to mellow the heat and intensify the floral characteristics of the chilli.

Brown Fish Stock

I am purposefully writing this recipe just as a method because the stocks I make are derived from the ingredients we have to hand. This is not to say that a stock should ever be used as a compost bin to discard mishandled ingredients.

To produce a great brown fish stock, work with the same species of fish and not a mixture. It's important not to wash your fish bones; soaking a fish frame (the skeleton) in water to 'purge off the blood' or wash away impurities is backward logic to me as it only dilutes any qualities that the fish frame has.

Fish frames that have been allowed to dry slightly overnight in a refrigerator will take on better colour – giving you greater flavour – and will not stick to the pan when browning. I have always been told to cut the eyes from the head as they bring cloudiness and imperfection to the final result, but it is that imperfection and cloudiness that brings viscosity, flavour and character to the stock. There are times, however, when a clear stock is required and the omission of eyes could be considered. Chopping the fish frame into four or five pieces will maximise the opportunity to caramelise the surface during browning.

Gills will always bring bitterness to a stock and should be discarded. The congealed blood that resides in the spine of the fish just below the head can be easily removed with a pair of fish pliers or tweezers and then rubbed with paper towel.

Heat enough ghee or neutral-flavoured oil in a wide, heavy-based pot over a high heat and wait until there is a light haze over the pan. Carefully distribute the fish frame (80 per cent) pieces around the base, don't overlap or overcrowd the pan. Work in batches if necessary. Once all the fish is browned, about 5 minutes, remove and set aside.

Keep the heat high, add the vegetables (15 per cent), such as shallots, garlic and celery and coat well with all the fish fat and caramelised scratchings from the base of the pan. Add any hard herbs and toasted aromatics, such as fennel seed, star anise or coriander.

Once the vegetables have coloured slightly and are beginning to soften, return the fish frames to the pan. Add enough cold water to just cover the ingredients.

Cook for 25–30 minutes over a medium–high heat without skimming until the stock has reduced by half and the liquid is thicker in texture and carries a beautiful tan colour. (This lack of skimming may go against what you are always instructed, but the impurities that rise to the surface have a lot of flavour and I prefer a less clear, more viscous and richly flavoured stock to one with less taste.)

Pass through a sieve for traditional stock requirements or through a mouli and give it a quick pulse in a food processor to bring more richness and density to the finished stock. You could also emulsify a knob of butter in the stock with a little lemon juice – it'll only need a warm piece of sourdough to take it to even greater heights.

Fresh Roe in Vegetable Preparations

Roe can be looked at in a number of different ways, but most commonly it is available in a salted, dried (and possibly smoked) form that can be grated or sliced over warm ingredients to impart seasoning, texture and loads of umami.

Years ago, working in the kitchen, we received mirror dory every second day as it was a popular menu item, and each one of the fish that we received that week was full of roe, so in three days we had in excess of 5 kg (11 lb) roe. I had thought to salt it but instead I cut the sack's membrane and scraped the contents out. The result gave me the actual roe itself. I placed all these scraped eggs into a sieve and rinsed off all the impurities. Using a whisk at this stage allowed me to pick up any loose pieces of membrane that might clump up when cooked. The end result was millions of tiny eggs that could be stirred into just about anything, from barbecued corn kernels, butter and stock to mayonnaise, or added to a fish pie mix.

Fish Black Pudding

Producing a fish black pudding (blood sausage) was something I wanted to do to fulfil my desire to find a recipe for every part of a fish. Little did I know it would be one of the most delicious recipes we have created.

MAKES 2 LARGE SAUSAGES

3 French shallots, finely diced
25 g (1 oz) butter
salt
¼ teaspoon freshly grated nutmeg
¼ teaspoon ground clove
¼ teaspoon freshly ground black pepper
150 ml (5 fl oz) thick (double/heavy) cream
100 g (3½ oz/1½ cups) fresh coarsely ground
    brioche breadcrumbs
100 ml (3½ fl oz) blood from a freshly caught wild
    kingfish/amberjack/Spanish mackerel (avoid tuna
    blood as the aroma is far too strong)
80 g (2¾ oz) ghee

Sweat the shallots in the butter in a saucepan over a gentle heat until completely tender, about 5 minutes. Season well with salt, add the spices and cook for 2 minutes, or until fragrant. Remove from the heat and add the cream. Leave until completely cool.

Add the brioche crumbs and fish blood and stir well to combine. It should resemble a thick batter consistency. Adjust the seasoning.

Spoon half the pudding mix into a square of plastic wrap that is still attached to the roll, then roll the pudding into a sausage as tight as you can and with as little air inside as possible. Repeat with the rest of the mix to make two sausages.

Bring a saucepan half full of water to the boil, then reduce the heat to 80–85°C (176–185°F) and poach the sausages for 25 minutes, or until they are firm to the touch and are fully cooked.

Plunge the sausages into a bowl of iced water and leave for 10 minutes, or until completely cold. Remove the plastic wrap carefully, cut the sausages into discs and pat dry with paper towel.

Heat the ghee in a wide-based frying pan and wait until there is a light haze over the pan. Carefully add a disc, cut side down, to the pan and fry for 1 minute on each side until coloured. Remove from the pan and season again lightly. Repeat with the rest of the discs.

This sausage is very versatile and can be used interchangeably for pig's blood pudding. The flavour profile is very mild due to the dairy and spice used – if anything, there is a mild taste of anchovy.

Fried Scales – Sweet & Savoury

Fish scales are wonderful little vehicles for flavour. On the opening menu at Saint Peter we fried red mullet scales and seasoned them with vinegar powder and ground fennel seeds, then sprinkled them over the top of a salt-roasted pumpkin. Texture is so important with softer ingredients like this and fish scales, if used in a considered way, can be a creative, delicious way to provide it.

Scale a smaller fish that has smaller scales, such as whiting, bream, red mullet or flathead. Place the scales in a small saucepan of cold water to cover and bring to the boil. Repeat this process 5 times, each time with new cold water. This will not only clean the scales but make them slightly more tender in the final product.

Meanwhile, pour 2 litres (68 fl oz/8 cups) canola (rapeseed) oil into a saucepan set over a medium-high heat. While this is coming up to the desired temperature of 185°C (365°F), make sure that the blanched scales are completely dry. Dust them very lightly in rice flour.

When the oil has reached a light haze and is 185°C (365°F), carefully add the scales and deep-fry for about 5 seconds, until crisp but without too much colour. Using a sieve, drain and set on paper towel to dry out. Season liberally with fine salt and set aside in a dry place ready for serving. You can add other flavours here too, such as ground fennel, togarashi, ground seaweed, etc.

When considering fish scales for sweet applications, at the point of boiling the scales in water 5 times, on the fifth time trade the water for a 60:40 sugar:water solution. This will give the scales a thin sugar coating that, when fried, will caramelise and have the potential for sweet applications.

Grilled Skewers of Offal & Intercostal

Grilling anything over charcoal is a sure-fire way of making food taste more savoury, smoky and, almost always, more delicious. There are quite a few recipes for offal in this book but these particular skewers bring smokiness and a touch of elegance to fairly rich ingredients. To offset the richness of heart, roe, spleen, liver or the intercostal (the meat that sits between the ribs), different flavours can be used as condiments to go with each piece.

1. INTERCOSTAL WITH ANCHOVY GARUM & LEMON

The discovery of this particular cut came about when taking the rib bones off a fillet of bass grouper. Like the meat that sits between the bones on a lamb rack, these delicious morsels of fatty, textural meat are not to be overlooked.

Once the strip of rib bones and flesh have been removed in one piece, cut the finger of meat that sits between each bone and set aside. (There is no need to remove the sinews as they will melt away during cooking.)

Thread on to a stainless-steel skewer or back on the cleaned rib bone that the meat has been cut from, then brush with ghee and season with sea salt. Place over a charcoal grill, barbecue plate or chargrill pan and cook for 30–40 seconds on each side. Remove from the heat and season liberally with Fish Garum (page 73), lemon juice and cracked black pepper.

Fish most suitable for this preparation are hapuka, sea bass, bass grouper, bar cod, Atlantic cod, most snappers and kingfish.

2. HEART & SPLEEN WITH A DROP OF FERMENTED CHILLI PASTE

Preheat a charcoal grill, barbecue or chargrill pan. Using a sharp knife, thinly slice 2 wild kingfish hearts and cut 2 wild kingfish spleens into quarters lengthways. Thread the spleen and heart pieces onto a long stainless-steel skewer. Season lightly with sea salt and brush with a little oil or ghee.

Make sure your charcoal grill, barbecue or chargrill pan is very hot, then grill for 20 seconds on the first side. Flip and cook the other side. The spleen should remain pink inside. Remove from the grill and squeeze a cheek of lemon over the flesh, then add a few drops of fermented chilli paste (see note) to taste. Serve.

Note: Fermented chilli paste is produced by burying long red chillies, which have been split in half, in rock salt and leaving them for 3 months. This softens the chilli and also sweetens the flavour. Gochujang (Korean red chilli paste) is a suitable substitute.

3. LIVER WITH LEMON JAM

Preheat a charcoal grill, barbecue or chargrill pan. Remove any visible arteries or minor blemishes from a large hapuka or sea bass liver, then pat dry. Cut the liver into 4 x 1 cm (1½ x ½ in) lengths and thread these on to long stainless-steel skewers. Season lightly with sea salt and brush with a little oil or ghee.

Make sure your charcoal grill, barbecue or chargrill pan is very hot, then grill for 20 seconds. Flip and cook the other side. Make sure the liver remains pink inside. Remove from the grill and squeeze a cheek of lemon over the flesh, then brush with a little good-quality store-bought (or, even better, home-made) lemon jam or marmalade to taste. Serve.

4. ROE WITH PEPPER & LIME

Preheat a charcoal grill, barbecue or chargrill pan. Fold and thread enough fish roe onto a long stainless-steel skewer to half-fill the skewer. (The roe cut from smaller species of fish like mullet, flathead or whiting are perfect for this method of cooking). Season lightly with sea salt and brush with a little oil or ghee.

Make sure your charcoal grill, barbecue or chargrill pan is very hot, then carefully grill for 20 seconds on each side, being particularly careful as you turn so as not to pop the membrane housing the eggs inside (the idea is to gently warm the roe and set it through). Remove from the grill and squeeze a cheek of lime over the warmed roe. Season liberally with finely ground pepperberry or combine equal amounts of sichuan pepper, ground juniper and black pepper and use to season. Serve.

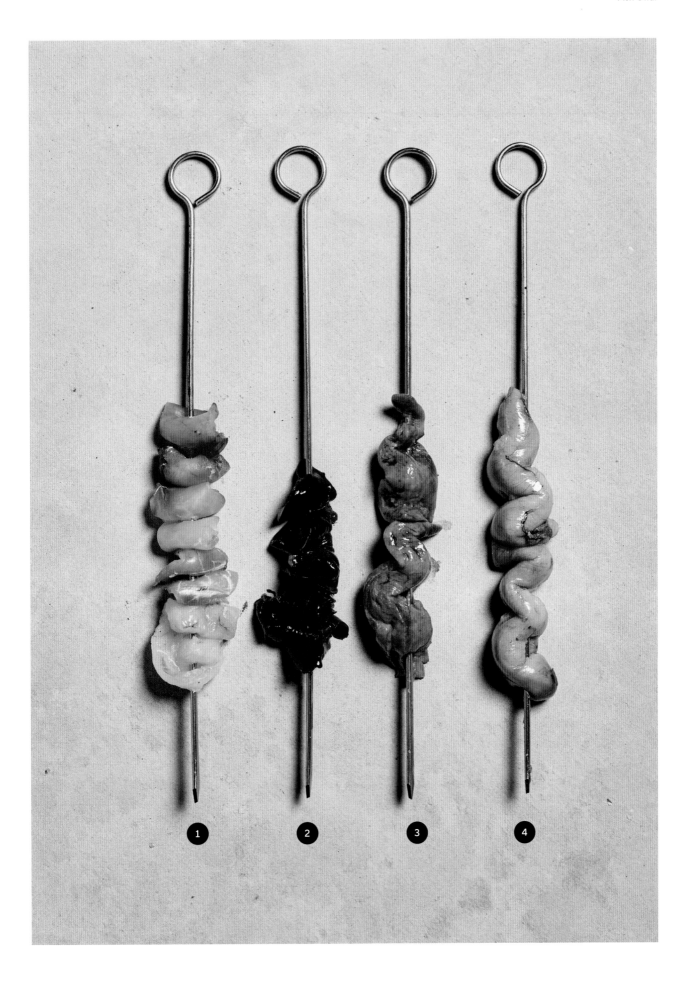

Milt Mortadella

This is a recipe that was brought to life by Paul Farag when we opened Fish Butchery, having started as an idea that I had but never had the opportunity to carry through. Paul and I still feel that there is more work to be done with this recipe so that we can achieve a particular consistency and flavour across a broader array of species.

MAKES 12–13 ENTRÉE PORTIONS

Milt base

80 g (2¾ oz/¼ cup) salt
1 litre (34 fl oz/4 cups) water
250 g (9 oz) skinless red gurnard fillet
250 g (9 oz) skinless cobia fillet (or use cod or bream)
150 g (5½ oz) fresh fish milt (Spanish mackerel or wild kingfish)

Seasonings & emulsifiers

80 g (2¾ oz) Murray cod fat, diced
20 g (¾ oz) fine salt
1 teaspoon freshly cracked black pepper
150 g (5½ oz) sliced pitted green olives
50 g (1¾ oz) skim milk power
10 g (¼ oz) powdered gelatine or xanthan gum

Freeze a jug blender from a high-powered blender or Thermomix to ensure it is completely cold (see note).

Mix the salt and water together in a clean bowl. Add the gurnard, cobia and milt and leave for 24 hours.

To cure the diced Murray cod fat, cover with fine salt and chill for 2 days.

Rinse the fish fillets and milt briefly to remove any excess salt, then bring the water to the boil in a small pan, remove from the heat, add the fat and poach for 10 seconds over a low heat. Remove and place over a double bowl of ice to chill completely. Set aside.

Keep the brined fish and milt separate in the freezer to keep it very chilled and firm, but NOT FROZEN.

Using the pre-chilled jug blender, blend each chilled fish to a fine paste. Once the gurnard and cobia pastes are blended combine them and return to the blender, then begin to feed in the chilled milt until emulsified. Once the mousse is emulsified remove from the blender and pass through a fine-mesh sieve to remove any sinews or imperfections.

Beat in all the seasonings and emulsifiers with a rubber spatula until combined. Chill the mix in a chilled bowl for about 20 minutes, then fold through the cured Murray cod fat.

Place the mixture on plastic wrap and roll into an airtight log. Poach in a temperature-controlled water bath at 85°C (185°F). The mortadella is cooked when the internal temperature reaches 65°C (140°F).

Remove and chill in iced water immediately until completely cold.

Refrigerate overnight and the following day slice thinly. Serve with other cured fish hams and sausages as a charcuterie plate or in a white bread sandwich with tomato sauce!

Notes: Temperature is very important as everything needs to be kept ice cold but not frozen. If you don't have a sous-vide machine then use a bain-marie instead.

Fish Garum

Given the amount of trimmings or discarded bones are variable to each fish, we have written this recipe to represent percentages needed to produce any amount that you have. Up to 60 per cent has always been considered the loss of a round fish. Once the fillets are removed, even from 1 or 2 kg (2 lb 3 oz or 4 lb 6 oz) of the fish, there is still so much left.

We tried a number of different ways, some that failed and some that showed potential, but eventually one of our chefs, Tristan, discovered this recipe, which produces a stable fish sauce that can be made from just about any fish waste.

To produce the garum, start by adding 50 per cent of water to the total amount of heads, bones and scraps you have from small fish, such as sardine, mackerel, anchovies or trevally, then to this total quantity add 20 per cent of fine salt. Mix together, transfer to a mason (kilner) jar, seal and place in a circulator bath set to 40°C (104°F). Leave for 7 days, stirring once daily. It is possible to produce a garum without a circulator bath but I would suggest investing in one if you intend to try to produce this sauce as fish waste can be temperamental. If you don't have one, then use a sterilised mason jar and store in a dark place at room temperature, stirring every day. Make sure that the gall bladder is removed as it will make the finished sauce extremely bitter. This recipe is versatile and can be adapted to produce scallop, prawn (shrimp) or cuttlefish garums.

Smoked Hearts, Spleens & Roe

These particular types of offal have a significantly short shelf life so if other methods can't be achieved in time, then heavily salt them and leave them to cure. As a fish only has one heart and one spleen, collect and salt them as you process fish through the week. Make sure the organs are as free from blood as possible and are firm without imperfections before salting.

In smoked and dried form, these offal can be grated over warm ingredients to showcase their robust savoury profile, such as grated over salt-roasted celeriac, used as a garnish on a rib of tuna or added to cold dishes. The flavour profile is in the realm of dried bonito flakes, anchovy and dried tuna (mojama).

5–6 kg (11–13¼ lb) hearts, spleens or roe of wild kingfish, hamachi or yellowtail
about 500 g (1 lb 2 oz/1¾ cups) good-quality fine salt, plus extra for salting the offal at the start
1 x 14 g (½ oz) soaked hickory or cherry wood puck

Cover the hearts, spleens or roe from the fish liberally with salt. Make sure they are completely covered. You can add other flavours here, such as citrus rinds, herbs or spices.

Using a clean plastic container, spread over enough salt to cover the base, then add the offal and cover with salt. Leave for 7 days, uncovered in the refrigerator. Then, using very clean hands, check for firmness. If they are still very soft then repeat the process with fresh salt for a further 4–5 days.

Once all the offal is firmly cured, remove and scrape each organ free from any salt sitting on the surface.

Cold smoke the offal in a smoker for 20–30 minutes depending on your desired degree of smokiness. Alternatively, line the top of a double steamer with foil, add soaked wood chips in the base and use this to cold smoke.

Preheat the oven to the lowest possible setting. Remove the offal from the smoker and place on a wire rack in a baking tray, then dry in the oven for up to 12 hours until completely dry. Leave to cool, then store in a sealed plastic container or vacuum-pack bags until needed.

Glazed Fish Throats

Renowned for its intense gelatinous quality, the Basque country hold this peculiar cut, which is known as *kokotxas* (and which I first came across when working in Paris) in high regard. Usually coming from either hake or cod, it is, in essence, the throat of the fish, an offcut taken from right under the gills. I like to cook it like this, or to simply lightly oil the flesh and season it with coarse sea salt, then grill over charcoal until the skin is sticky and flesh is soft.

SERVES 4

8 coral trout throats
150 ml (5 fl oz) verjuice
60 g (2 oz) butter
pinch of salt
1 tarragon sprig

Place the fish throats in a small frying pan and add all the ingredients, then cover them with baking paper. Bring to a gentle simmer for 12 minutes, or until the liquid reduces resulting in a sticky glaze around the cooked throats. Either eat the throat with a fillet from the same fish or by itself with peas that have been cooked with a splash of stock, extra-virgin olive oil, tarragon and plenty of black pepper.

FISHUES

Sometimes, even when we go to the effort of sourcing excellent quality fish, things can go wrong. It's for this reason that I've included this list of 'fishues' – issues that can occur when dealing with fish, all of which I have had to face at some point or another. These include things such as why a fish sometimes curls dramatically in a pan, why it can be rendered to complete mush or why it just smells 'fishy'. The fear of serving a customer tough, mushy, milky, smelly or overcooked fish terrifies me, and it's something that I'm constantly testing and checking on a daily basis. Here is some key advice for each of these potential problems.

1. 'Fishy' fish

Fish flesh contains an odourless chemical known as trimethylamine-N-oxide, or TMAO. Once a fish is killed and exposed to the air, the chemical breaks down into derivatives of ammonia and smells 'fishy'. TMAO is used as an indicator of how fresh a fish is and the smell, it is said, can be reduced in two ways.

First: 'The surface of the fish can be rinsed off with tap water'.

This statement is counter-productive. Fish is like a sponge and will absorb unnecessary moisture and washing the flesh can be detrimental to its shelf life, texture and flavour profile, making it extremely difficult to achieve good cooked results. It is for this reason that I advocate dry handling of fish throughout the preparation and storage processes (see page 27).

Second: 'Treating the fish with acidic ingredients, such as lemon, vinegar or tomato can also cause TMAO to bind to water and become less volatile... thus, the odour compounds do not reach the nose'.

As a chef, I find this fascinating as it explains why globally a lemon wedge appears next to most seafood dishes. Think about it, the fish dishes we all love include acid – yes, to bring balance and additional flavour, but also to mask any odour that may be present. The vinegar in hollandaise sauce, the white wine in beurre blanc, the capers and cornichons in tartare sauce and the king of fish dishes, bouillabaisse – full of tomatoes and wine. These are all acid-forward dishes. Now, I'll be the first person to express the joy I get in eating a perfectly grilled piece of whiting in beurre blanc, but I'm also fascinated that through correct handling and storing of fish, alternate flavour profiles can be built promoting more complex savoury flavours. This gives us the opportunity not only to work with a fish for a longer period of time but allows us to pair it with less acidic garnishes, such as mushrooms, chestnuts and onions, which frame fish in a different light.

2. Tough fish

Tough Fish Syndrome (TFS) is exhibited by certain tropical reef fish, and some other fish varieties, in which the texture of the flesh toughens severely after cooking, rendering the fish inedible. Prior to this point the fish is not visually different to any other fish – the fish fillet and the raw flesh has similar texture to that of non-tough fish, but upon cooking, a 'tough' fish will have a texture that is described as 'extremely rubbery'.

As well as TFS causing fish to buckle and curl when cooked, poor handling of a fish by the fisherman can also result in a similar issue.

If purchasing a fish known to be affected by TFS, make sure to always cut a section from the tail and cook it before scaling, gutting or filleting (see left). This way you will know that the fish is in good or bad condition. Unfortunately, if you do come across a fish with TFS there is no way to combat this issue – you could park a car on top of the fillet while pan-frying it, but the texture will be tough and useless even after this. My only suggestion would be to cure (see page 57) or cold smoke an affected fish.

3. Mushy fish

Kudoa thyrsites are parasites that embed themselves into the gills of some marine fish. The reason for bringing this particular parasite into the conversation is to shine a light on a fairly unknown reason as to why some fish are mushy post-cooking. This is an issue not only isolated to Australian waters but one that affects a majority of species globally. Although the parasite is not dangerous to humans it poses a major issue for fisheries and market

Testing, testing

I am always diligent when purchasing fish that, regardless of species, I will cut the first portion out of the tail while it is still on the bone and cook it all the way through, so I can see how the flesh stands up to the heat. If the muscle composition remains intact and the flesh is firm, even when cooked well done, then you have a good fish. Conversely, it'll be clear if you have a fish that is affected by Tough Fish Syndrome or one that suffers from a parasite that causes the flesh to turn mushy.

Cooking a section of any fish needs to be a priority to not only chefs around the world but for all of us who want to have good experiences with fish. Cooking a piece of fish and eating it yourself before sharing it with others will give you the reassurance that you are handling a good fish, and you will be able to make better choices with what sides to accompany the fish as well as working out what method of cookery to apply.

spaces that sell affected fish to the unknowing consumer who then cooks and serves it and has a poor fish experience.

For the years I have been handling fish, this has been a common problem that I've faced with species ranging from wild kingfish, mahi-mahi and Spanish mackerel; the moment that heat is applied, the structure of the flesh begins to soften and collapse. A number of chefs I have worked with have questioned why I would buy a wild kingfish that could be mushy over a farmed kingfish that is consistently fatty and firm. I know in my experience that although you run the risk of buying a mushy fish, you also stand a good chance of eating a fish that is unrivalled in flavour and texture.

Sadly, there is no way to know whether your fish is affected by this issue until you have cooked it, so I suggest testing a section of the fish before cooking the remainder.

4. Raw fish that looks cooked

There have been a number of times where I've cut into an externally beautiful looking fish only to notice that the flesh looks as though it had already been cooked. The muscles seemed as if they were opening up and almost weeping a lot of moisture and the red muscle or lateral line of the fish was completely oxidised and spoilt. The cause of this is a build-up of lactic acid 'burning' the muscle of the fish in a similar way to that in which citrus cooks the flesh of fish for ceviche.

At both Saint Peter and Fish Butchery we work with a number of fishermen who catch fish on the line and follow a traditional Japanese technique known as *iki jime* (where fish is immediately brain spiked and ice slurried). When done correctly, this technique brings on rigor mortis and, as a result, reduces any chance of lactic acid building up in the muscle of the fish – in turn preserving its best texture and potential flavour profile.

The only way to check for the problem of lactic acid build-up is by looking at the condition of the flesh of the fish. If there is any doubt, cook the fillet first. If the fillet drops a lot of moisture through cooking and there is noticeable protein (white spots) weeping from the muscle of the fish then it is best to avoid serving it. Contact the store where you purchased the fish so they are aware of the issue.

5. Overcooked fish

It is said that there are mere seconds between undercooking and overcooking a fish. To a degree this is true, but cooking a fillet of fish in a pan on the highest heat until it's completely cooked doesn't put you in a good place for excellent results. A fish can be cooked a number of ways – selecting the method that matches the species is often the most challenging part of fish cookery.

For example, poaching fish is a far more forgiving medium than pan-frying, as there is a little more control over the heat. The same can be said for crumbing fish. A crumbed fish is perfect for the amateur cook, as the crumb provides insulation and protection to the flesh while cooking, which, in turn, creates a wonderful crunchy exterior and a just set, moist interior that showcases the fish's sweetness and firmness perfectly. Even if the fish gets a little too cooked or extra crispy around the edges, it will still be delicious... you might just need a little extra Yoghurt tartare sauce (see page 144).

If you are a novice at cooking fish, or even someone who has had some practice, then invest in a probe thermometer.

THE

RECIPES

RAW, CURED & PICKLED

Great fish for raw/cured/pickled
preparations include:

Albacore

Alfonsino

Anchovies

Arctic char

Blue mackerel

Bonito

Garfish

Gurnard

Sardines

Sea bream

Sea bass (Branzino)

Snapper (including Red snapper)

Trevally

Tuna

Whiting

Yellowtail

The key to an excellent raw fish dish is the texture and flavour of the fish itself. Ageing, curing, pickling, brining and partially cooking can help unlock unique textures and flavours, but the beauty of raw, cured or pickled fish is that, if the fish is well handled, then few ingredients are needed to make it taste better than itself in its most natural form.

Personally, when cutting fish for eating raw I always consider whether to cut from the flesh side or skin side and whether to start at the tail or shoulder end, as these choices will result in a different textural profile. (Even now, when working with a fish that I have yet to prepare, I will start by cutting it a number of different ways to find the most suitable texture I am looking for.) Once I have determined the mouthfeel of the fish I then consider what process to apply. Do I serve it as is, dressed with a fruity extra-virgin olive oil? Maybe I season it now and serve it in 30 minutes, giving it time to firm the flesh up a little? Should I cure this fish to give it a ham-like texture or would smoking make it taste even more delicious?

The bottom line is to keep things simple and only do what is necessary – nothing more. The following recipes feature some simple preparations and ideas for raw, cured and pickled fish that can be applied to a wide variety of fish species.

Left, overleaf & page 86: Spangled emperor.

RAW FISH ESSENTIALS

Eating raw fish is not for everyone, but for me it is a clean, honest way of getting to taste what the fish is like, while dressings and seasoning are key to heightening the subtle flavours that are present.

1.

TO ALTER TEXTURES AND APPEARANCE IN RAW FISH. Consider leaving the skin of the fish on to serve. For example, place your chosen fish fillet on a wire rack, skin side up, then shock the skin with three generous ladles (250 ml/8½ fl oz/1 cup) of boiling hot water. This will gently soften the skin to a texture that is palatable. Another method is to lightly oil the skin of a fish fillet, then place a square of baking paper on the base of a very hot cast-iron pan and carefully place the fillet, skin side down, on the paper. Count to five, firmly holding the fillet flat to the pan, then remove from the pan. This intense burst of heat will bring smokiness, firmness and palatability to the skin.

2.

CEVICHE OR THE USE OF ACID. This is very popular as it is an efficient and delicious method of cookery. However, lime juice (traditionally used in ceviche preparations) begins to degenerate the proteins in fish within seconds of being added and takes it from raw to cooked. Using other acidic ingredients, such as verjuice, oxidised wine and fermented juices, allows us to season the fish with liquor derived from fermentation for acidity, but won't damage the flesh as quickly as citric juices.

3.

DRY-AGEING OF FISH (SEE PAGE 29). This helps heighten nuances of flavour that are present in raw fish, which can be undetectable on days one, two and three. The best example of this is eating yellowfin tuna on day three right through to day thirty-six. When left on the bone to mature in a controlled environment, the flavour of the tuna can dramatically transform from having a firm, slightly sweet and briny texture to a more compact dense one with the aromas of mushroom and cured tuna (mojama).

Sardines & Anchovies in Lemon Thyme Oil

If you can find ultra-fresh sardines and anchovies then this recipe is a must. It is critical to the texture and flavour of the fish that they are served warm, not cold, and still be raw, not cooked. To have both these beautiful fish together on one plate is more significant in my eyes than seeing truffle and foie gras together.

SERVES 4

10 fresh whole sardines
10 fresh whole anchovies
sea salt flakes and freshly cracked
    black pepper

Lemon thyme oil
500 ml (17 fl oz/2 cups) good-quality
    extra-virgin olive oil
2 tablespoons lemon thyme leaves or
    native thyme leaves

To prepare the sardines, if right handed, start with the sardine head on your left off the chopping board, tail to the right and the backbone facing you. I fillet these sardines with the gut in as it is too time consuming to remove beforehand. Make a small cut behind the head, separating the fish collar from the rest of the fillet. This gives you access to make a clean cut down the frame of the fish removing the fillet intact in one movement of the knife from the head to tail. The first fillet of the fish is simpler to remove as you have the support of the bottom fillet to rest on. The second is trickier, but use the chopping board for support. The fish don't require pin boning, but cut the rib bones out of the sardines with a small knife.

Fillet the remaining sardines and anchovies. Don't discard the bones, heads or gut of the fish as they can be made into garum (see page 73).

For the oil, I prefer to use a Thermomix, but if you don't have one, bring the oil and thyme leaves to 85°C (185°F) in a small saucepan, then blitz in a blender until fragrant. If using a Thermomix, set it at 85°C (185°F) and blend on high for 10 minutes until fragrant. Pass through a sieve lined with muslin (cheesecloth).

Arrange five of the anchovies on a warmed serving plate, then place the sardines on top. Repeat with a second plate. Season to taste and pour over enough of the oil to cover the plates generously. Lemon juice can be added to offset the oiliness of the dish but make sure there's plenty of crusty bread to eat these beautiful fish with.

ALTERNATIVE FISH:
Herring
Mackerel
Trevally

Marinated Silver Trevally & Lemon Verjuice

This dish puts into practice the thinking that verjuice can be used as an acidic ingredient to firm up the texture and help enhance the wonderful natural oils of silver trevally. To make the lemon verjuice, some simple planning is needed.

SERVES 4

4 boneless silver trevally or mullet
  fillets, skin on
sea salt

Lemon verjuice

250 g (9 oz) whole Meyer lemon or
  bergamot, or yuzu when in season
2 litres (68 fl oz/8 cups) good-quality
  verjuice
2 tablespoons caster (superfine) sugar
pinch of salt

Verjuice dressing

2 teaspoons coriander seeds
pinch of salt
1 teaspoon caster (superfine) sugar
2 large banana shallots, finely sliced
  into rings
140 ml (4½ fl oz) extra-virgin olive oil
80 ml (2½ fl oz/⅓ cup) Lemon verjuice
  (see above)

For the lemon verjuice, place the fruit together with the remaining ingredients in a sterilised mason (kilner) jar. Seal and chill for at least 7 days until the flavours have developed. Strain into a clean jar and chill until needed.

For the dressing, toast the coriander seeds in a small frying pan over a medium heat until fragrant and lightly toasted. Cool, then crack the seeds in a mortar and pestle. Combine the cracked coriander seeds, salt, sugar and shallot and set aside for at least 30 minutes, preferably overnight, then stir in the oil and verjuice. Set aside.

To prepare the fish, ensure there are no scales or bones on the flesh. Turn the fish onto the flesh side so the skin side is facing upwards. Using your fingers, grab on to the corner of the skin closest to where the head would have been and pull the skin gently off the flesh leaving behind the 'silver skin'. Cut the fillets into thickish slices and arrange on a small plate. Season well with sea salt.

Lightly dress the fish with the dressing, making sure some of the coriander seeds and shallot are distributed over each plate. Serve at room temperature. For a slightly more substantial plate, the addition of crisp peppery leaves, such as witlof (endive/chicory), rocket (arugula) or radish would go perfectly.

ALTERNATIVE FISH:
Anchovies
Mackerel
Sardines

Raw Red Snapper, Green Almonds, Fig Leaf Oil & Garum

Native Australian red snapper, also known as nannygai, is renowned for its firm texture and sweet, shellfish-like quality. This is a fish that's far more interesting texturally and holds far more flavour than stock standard snapper.

Spring in Australia means green almonds and they are among my favourite ingredients. Juicy, acidic and with a little crunch, they go perfectly with raw fish dishes.

SERVES 4

2 boneless red snapper (nannygai), bream or snapper fillets, skin on
300 g (10½ oz/2 cups) fresh green almonds (see note)
100 ml (3½ fl oz) Fish Garum (see page 73) or good-quality fish sauce, white soy sauce or light soy sauce
100 ml (3½ fl oz) Fig leaf oil (see below)
juice of 1 lime

Fig leaf oil

125 g (4½ oz) fresh fig leaves or use kaffir lime leaves or bay leaves
250 ml (8½ fl oz/1 cup) extra-virgin olive oil

For the fig leaf oil, trim the fig leaf off the central stem and discard, then place the leaves and oil into a Thermomix set to 85°C (185°F) and blend on high for 10 minutes. Place a bowl inside a larger bowl of ice. Strain the oil through a filter paper-lined sieve into the chilled bowl. Transfer to an airtight container and chill in the freezer until needed. If you don't have a Thermomix, bring the fig leaves and oil to 85°C (185°F) in a pan. Transfer to a blender and blend on low speed, then gradually increase the speed and blend for 5–6 minutes until the oil is flavoured.

To prepare the fish, bring a small saucepan of water to the boil over a high heat.

Using a sharp knife, make eight slashes in the skin – just cutting the skin but not going deep into the flesh – then arrange the fish over a wire rack. Using a 50 ml (1¾ fl oz) ladle, tip three ladlefuls of boiling water over the skin of each fillet. Transfer the rack to the refrigerator and leave to dry for at least 30 minutes.

For the green almonds, use a small, sharp knife to cut the nut in half lengthways, then carefully take the tender green almond out by cracking the outer shell to help it fall out or by flicking it out with the tip of the knife. Set aside.

To cut the fish, working from the head to the tail, cut 5 mm (¼ in) thick slices from the fillet. You will need about eight slices per portion, about 75–80 g (2¾ oz) each. Assemble these on a serving plate, then dress the fish with the garum, fig leaf oil and lime juice. Serve at room temperature.

Note: Peel the green almonds and use them immediately as they are prone to oxidising and going brown (a way to avoid this oxidisation if the plan is to peel them ahead of time is to store them in milk). The oil here is best made in this quantity so you have enough to blend – the excess will freeze well and is good for salad dressings, with roast pork or brushed over cooked fish.

ALTERNATIVE FISH:
Albacore
Sea bass
Sea bream

Wild Kingfish & Roe Dressing

Sauce gribiche is a traditional French cold egg sauce and is the inspiration for this dressing, which is made from cooked fish roe, capers, cornichons, parsley, chervil, tarragon and extra-virgin olive oil. There is something quite special about getting the eggs and raw fillet of the same fish on one plate. It shows technique and a multitude of textures and flavours, while also respecting the whole fish. A number of alternate fish species can be used in this recipe, such as john dory, coral trout, yellowtail kingfish, Murray cod and rainbow runner.

SERVES 4

400 g (14 oz) boneless wild kingfish
    fillet, skin on

Roe dressing

250 g (9 oz) fresh roe, scraped from
    the membrane
500 ml (17 fl oz/2 cups) extra-virgin
    olive oil
½ tablespoon dijon mustard
½ tablespoon chardonnay vinegar or
    white-wine vinegar with a pinch of
    sugar
1 bunch chervil, finely chopped
½ bunch tarragon, finely chopped
30 g (1 oz/¼ cup) capers, drained and
    finely chopped
90 g (3 oz/½ cup) cornichons, drained
    and finely diced
sea salt flakes and freshly cracked
    black pepper

For the dressing, add the scraped fish roe to a pan and cover with the olive oil. Stir over a very low heat for 10 minutes, or until the eggs have cooked evenly, then strain the roe into a bowl, reserving 250 ml (8½ fl oz/1 cup) of the cooking oil, and chill for 20–30 minutes.

Add the mustard and vinegar to the chilled roe, then stir in the reserved cooking olive oil, drop by drop, adding a little vinegar or warm water, if necessary, until thick and creamy. Add the chopped herbs, capers and cornichons and season to taste. Set aside.

Position the fillet so it is skin side down and the head of the fillet is facing you. Using a sharp knife, put the blade of the knife between the skin and flesh and, keeping the angle of the knife positioned down towards the skin, force the blade along the length of the skin working towards the tail. You should try and leave as much of the red muscle as possible behind, as it carries a lot of the flavour and natural oils.

Once the skin is removed, turn the fish so that it is red muscle-side up and separate the top loin from the belly by following the lateral line of the fillet. Place a spoonful of the dressing in the centre of a bowl, then arrange slices of the fish neatly within the dressing. Season the fish lightly with sea salt and serve.

ALTERNATIVE FISH:
Amberjack
John dory
Rainbow runner

Raw Diced Yellowfin Tuna, Sour Onions, Egg Yolk & Endive

Ageing the yellowfin tuna here to anywhere between day seven and nine will promote a more savoury characteristic that will help in executing this version of a steak tartare. If working with a section of tuna that isn't from the centre of the loin, use a spoon to scrape away the flesh from the sinews and use this meat instead of the diced fish.

SERVES 3

250 g (9 oz) trimmed centre cut
    yellowfin tuna loin (ideally aged
    7–9 days)
2 banana shallots, finely diced
80 g (2¾ oz) shop-bought pickled
    onions, diced
1 bunch chives, finely chopped
2 egg yolks
60 ml (2 fl oz/¼ cup) good-quality
    extra-virgin olive oil
2 tablespoons pickled onion juice
    from the jar
sea salt flakes and freshly cracked
    black pepper
2 yellow witlof (endive/chicory)
    heads, leaves separated

Dice the tuna into 1 x 1 cm (½ in) cubes and place in a large bowl (be sure to wear disposable gloves here to avoid contamination). Add the shallots, pickled onions, chives and an egg yolk and mix well to combine. Add enough olive oil to coat all the ingredients well, then enough pickled onion juice to bring the desired amount of acidity. Season well with salt and pepper.

Assemble the mixture on a plate with witlof leaves surrounding the fish and top with the remaining egg yolk. Thin slices of crisp sourdough are also great additions to this dish.

ALTERNATIVE FISH:
Albacore
Trevally
Swordfish

Salt & Vinegar Blue Mackerel & Cucumbers with Fried Rye Bread

This dish of blue mackerel and cucumber is the perfect demonstration of how pickling can transform the texture and flavour of a fish. Any cucumber would be great here, but I particularly enjoy it with apple white cucumbers as they have an oyster-like characteristic that goes so well with the mackerel. The fried bread will need to be prepared ahead of time as it needs to be dried overnight before frying.

SERVES 4

4 very fresh boneless blue mackerel fillets (about 80 g/2¾ oz each)
80 g (2¾ oz/⅔ cup) sea salt flakes
250 ml (8½ fl oz/1 cup) sherry vinegar
4 cracked juniper berries
2 apple white or Lebanese (short) cucumbers
8 freshly shucked rock oysters, any brine reserved (optional)
100 ml (3½ fl oz) good-quality extra-virgin olive oil

Fried rye bread

1.2 litres (41 fl oz) full-cream (whole) milk
3 banana shallots, finely diced
1 bay leaf
3 thyme sprigs
1 x 500 g (1 lb 2 oz) loaf of day-old rye bread (any sourdough bread), crusts removed and cut into 5 cm (2 in) cubes
fine salt
1 litre (34 fl oz/4 cups) canola (rapeseed) or cottonseed oil, for frying

Preheat the oven to its lowest setting. Line two baking trays with baking paper.

For the fried rye bread, bring the milk, shallots, bay leaf and thyme to a simmer in a saucepan over a medium heat. Remove from the heat, add the bread cubes and cover with baking paper. Leave for 20 minutes, or until the bread is very soft, then transfer to a food processor and blend until very smooth. Very thinly spread the bread paste over the prepared baking trays from edge to edge, then leave them in the oven to dry overnight.

The next day, heat the oil for frying in a large saucepan over a medium–high heat until the temperature reaches 170°C (340°F). Snap a square of the bread crisp off the tray and deep-fry for 20 seconds, or until golden and crisp. Drain on paper towel and season with a few salt flakes, then fry the rest of the bread. Set aside in a warm, dry place until needed (they are best used within 1 hour of frying).

To pickle the mackerel, season the skin and flesh side evenly with the salt, then place on a tray and refrigerate, uncovered, for 2 hours.

Once the time has passed, submerge the fish in a bath of the vinegar and juniper berries and leave to chill for 30 minutes.

Meanwhile, to prepare the cucumbers, peel the thick outer skin and dice the flesh into 1 x 1 cm (½ in) cubes, avoiding the seeds.

Remove the pickled mackerel from the vinegar, reserving the vinegar. Turn the fish onto the flesh side so it is skin side facing up. Using your fingers, grab on to the corner of the skin closest to where the head would have been and pull the skin gently off the flesh leaving behind the 'silver skin'. Slice the mackerel thickly, about 1 cm (½ in) from the head to the tail. Assemble these on serving plates, add two oysters to each plate, if using, and sprinkle over the cucumber, oyster brine and a few drops of the juniper-flavoured vinegar. Dress with a little olive oil and serve with the fried rye bread.

ALTERNATIVE FISH:
Bonito
Garfish
Yellowtail bugfish

Selection of Aged, Cured & Smoked Fish Hams & Gherkins

This dish is more a way of putting together the fish hams on pages 58–61. Like any good charcuterie board, gherkins, cornichons or pickles are a great way of bringing acidity to rich ingredients, and these lacto-fermented cucumbers are fantastic for serving with cured and smoked fish. They are so versatile – give them a try and they'll soon become a pantry staple.

SERVES 6

100 g (3½ oz) Paul's Spiced Marlin
   Ham on the Bone (see page 58)
100 g (3½ oz) Cured & Smoked Brown
   Trout (see page 60)
100 g (3½ oz) Moonfish Guanciale
   (see page 61)
100 g (3½ oz) Swordish Bacon
   (see page 60)

Lacto-fermented cucumbers

90 g (3 oz/⅓ cup) fine salt
3 litres (101 fl oz/12 cups) water
1 tablespoon toasted fennel seeds
2 tablespoons whole black
   peppercorns
2 garlic cloves, crushed
1 kg (2 lb 3 oz) small pickling
   cucumbers

For the fermented cucumbers, combine the salt, water, fennel seeds, peppercorns and garlic in a very clean large bowl with a pouring lip and stir until the salt is completely dissolved.

Wash the cucumbers thoroughly to remove any debris, then place them inside a large sterilised mason (kilner) jar. Pour the brine over the cucumbers and place a small square of baking paper on top to keep the contents submerged. Seal and leave to ferment in a cool place for at least 4–5 weeks before consuming. Once opened, store in the refrigerator.

Using a very sharp knife, thinly slice the ham, cured and smoked brown trout, guanciale and the bacon, making sure to trim away the skin of the fish if they are still on. Assemble on baking paper on a board or plate and leave to stand to make sure they are at room temperature before serving.

Serve the sliced meats alongside hot crusty baguette, chilled good-quality butter and the fermented cucumbers.

ALTERNATIVE FISH:
Bonito
Kingfish
Tuna

See photo on following pages.

POACHED

Great fish for poaching
preparations include:

Arctic char

Bass grouper

Blue-eye trevalla

Gurnard

Haddock

Hapuka

Kingfish

Murray cod

Plaice

Pollock

Spanish mackerel

Snapper

Turbot

Trout

For some reason poaching has fallen out of fashion with fish in favour of more desirable methods of cookery such as frying, roasting and sous-vide. The reason for this, I believe, is the perception that poaching is seen to be a little tricky, or that it's lacking in texture and flavour.

Poaching can be a very healthy way of cooking if using either water or stock along with flavourful aromatics, such as herbs and spices, to bring subtle flavours to the fish. On the other side though, poaching in butter or fats is an extremely decadent way to enjoy a variety of fish species.

Being a wet method of cookery, poaching aids in moisture retention and has the ability to directly penetrate flavours into the fish. The potential of different poaching liquids is endless. Next time you're working with a liquid, consider what flavour it could impart into a fish. I've had fantastic results with the brine strained from green olives, the whey strained from ricotta cheese and even the liquid strained from cooked mushrooms.

Left, overleaf & page 108: Blue-eye trevalla (aged 2 days).

POACHED FISH ESSENTIALS

The basic method for poaching below gives you so much flexibility to adapt flavours and ingredients, species to species. As you feel more confident with this method, dishes, such as the fish curry, fish soup and head terrine, will be possible.

1.

Bring a lidded saucepan of stock and aromatics to the boil. Once boiling, remove from the heat and set aside on the work surface. Uncover and, using a probe thermometer, cool the liquid to 85°C (185°F). Very carefully as the liquid is hot, place a small saucer and the fish into the base of the pan. Cover with the lid and cook with the pan off the heat for 6 minutes depending on the thickness and species of fish.

2.

Use a slotted spoon to remove the fish to a clean plate. Rest for 4 minutes, skin side up, then gently peel away the skin – the skin peeling off easily is an indicator that the flesh is cooked, or at least almost cooked. (Why wouldn't you eat the fish skin on? Given the poaching liquid gets as low as 65°C (149°F) during cooking the skin of some fish species will still be tough and rubbery.)

NOTE: Don't throw away the skin, add it back to the pan of poaching liquid as this is your 'master stock' to continue poaching in. The gelatine present in the skin is a thickener and will give the stock great viscosity. After a few fish are poached in this liquid it converts into a wonderful fish soup or sauce to spoon over the poached fish. At the end of each use, bring the liquid, skin or any sediment within the poaching stock to the boil then pass through a sieve. It freezes well.

3.

Serve the fish on a plate and ladle 100 ml (3½ fl oz) of the stock over it along with good extra-virgin olive oil and sea salt flakes.

Poached Hapuka, Artichokes & Garlic Mayonnaise

As an apprentice I would eat out in Sydney's restaurants as frequently as I could, and whole paycheques at times would be blown on extravagant meals. During that time of exploration, one of the best dishes I tried was a simple poached kingfish with artichokes cooked in sauce barigoule at the wonderful restaurant Bistrode (quite possibly one of my all-time favourite places). Here is my interpretation of that wonderful plate of food.

SERVES 6

6 x 180 g (6½ oz) hapuka, bass
    grouper or bar cod fillets, skin on
    and pin-boned

Barigoule

1 tablespoon coriander seeds
½ tablespoon fennel seeds
½ tablespoon black peppercorns
1 fresh bay leaf
4 thyme sprigs
300 ml (10 fl oz) extra-virgin olive oil
½ onion, finely sliced
½ carrot, finely sliced
½ celery heart stalk, finely sliced
½ garlic bulb
500 ml (17 fl oz/2 cups) dry
    white wine
500 ml (17 fl oz/2 cups) water
1 kg (2 lb 3 oz) Jerusalem
    artichokes, halved

Garlic mayonnaise

2 egg yolks
½ tablespoon dijon mustard
2 teaspoons white-wine vinegar
fine salt
250 ml (8½ fl oz/1 cup) grapeseed oil
juice of ½ lemon
3 garlic cloves, finely grated

To serve (optional)

½ bunch each French tarragon,
    flat-leaf (Italian) parsley and
    chervil, leaves picked
3 sorrel leaves, sliced
½ bunch dill, sprigs picked

For the barigoule, tie the spices and herbs together in a muslin cloth (cheesecloth) to make a bouquet garni.

Heat the olive oil in a large, wide-based saucepan and cook the onion, carrot, celery and garlic for 7 minutes until tender, without colouring. Add the wine and bouquet garni and bring to the boil. Add the water and return to the boil, then set aside.

For the mayonnaise, rest a bowl on a tea towel (dish towel) draped over a saucepan to stabilise it. Add the egg yolks, mustard, vinegar and salt to the bowl and whisk to combine well. Continue whisking, slowly drizzling in the grapeseed oil to form a thick emulsion. Taste and add extra salt, the lemon juice and garlic to taste. It should be the thickness of softly whipped cream, so adjust with a little warm water if necessary. Set aside.

Place 500 ml (17 fl oz/2 cups) of the barigoule liquid and the cooked vegetables in a large saucepan and set aside. Place the remaining barigoule liquid in a large, heavy-based lidded pan and bring to the boil. Add the artichokes and cook until tender, then remove with a slotted spoon and set aside.

Remove the pan from the heat, add the fish, cover and set aside for 7–8 minutes until the flesh is just opaque. Using a slotted spoon, carefully remove the fish to a plate and gently peel away the skin (see page 109).

Combine the tarragon, parsley, chervil, sorrel and dill, if using, and set aside.

Bring the reserved 500 ml (17 fl oz/2 cups) barigoule liquid and all the vegetables, including the artichokes, to a simmer and spoon over the fish. Add a generous tablespoon of the mayonnaise and serve with the reserved herbs.

Notes: Traditionally a barigoule is used to poach and preserve artichokes. This stock has a generous layer of oil on top of it, but don't discard it, as it acts as a vinaigrette for the dish. The aromatics and vegetables also make a beautiful garnish for the finished dish.

ALTERNATIVE FISH:
Arctic char
Bass grouper
Hake

Bonito Poached in Fragrant Oil, BBQ Fennel Dressing & Crisp Potato

Oil-poaching is such an enjoyable way to eat bonito, tuna, mackerel or sardines. Bonito seems to be my favourite though, as there's something about the way the flesh slips off the muscle when perfectly cooked. When in season, bonito has a clean, briny flavour and quite a firm, dense texture that's best eaten raw or very lightly cooked. The use of fennel and aniseed is an obvious pairing with fish, but I love this dressing. By grilling the raw fennel, it breaks down the fibrous parts of the vegetable while still keeping it crunchy. In this recipe I have used ground kelp that we dry at the restaurant, but you can use ground wakame, konbu or nori instead. Note too that this needs to be started a day ahead.

SERVES 4

1 fillet cut from a large bonito, about 1.5–3 kg (3 lb 5 oz–6 lb 10 oz), skin on
1 litre (34 fl oz/4 cups) extra-virgin olive oil
100 g (3½ oz/1 cup) whole dried cracked black pepper
1 bay leaf
small handful juniper berries
small bunch rosemary
salt

Potato crisps

2 large waxy potatoes, such as desiree
pinch of salt
canola (rapeseed) oil, for deep-frying

Fennel dressing

1 large fennel bulb, tops intact
170 ml (5½ fl oz/⅔ cup) extra-virgin olive oil
80 g (2¾ oz) ground dried kelp
pinch of salt
1 teaspoon caster (superfine) sugar
60 g (2 oz) French shallots, finely sliced into rings
50 ml (1¾ fl oz) chardonnay vinegar or white-wine vinegar with a pinch of sugar

ALTERNATIVE FISH:
Albacore
Tuna
Swordfish

For the potato crisps, preheat the oven to its lowest setting. Peel the potatoes and, using a box grater, grate the potatoes into a large pan. Include all the starchy pulp too. Cover the potato with cold water and a good pinch of salt, then bring to the boil. Cook for 20 minutes, or until they are extremely soft and the liquid has thickened.

Using a mesh spoon, remove the thick pulp from the pan, leaving behind the starchy liquid. Blend the pulp in a blender to the consistency of thick (double/heavy) cream. If it is too thick, add a little of the starchy liquid to thin.

Line a baking tray with baking paper, then spread the potato puree thinly across the surface from edge to edge. Leave to dry in the oven overnight. The end result should be a thin, translucent chip.

The next day, half-fill a heavy-based saucepan with the oil for deep-frying and heat until the temperature reaches 180°C (350°F). Fry the potato crisp for 10–15 seconds until a light tan colour. Remove and drain on paper towel. Season and set aside.

To make the fennel dressing, using a mandoline or a very sharp knife, finely slice the fennel starting at the head and cutting down to the base. Add 30 ml (1 fl oz) of olive oil and toss until it is lightly dressed.

Using either a barbecue plate set to high or a cast-iron pan set over a high heat, add a little of the fennel in a single layer and grill for 1–2 minutes, turning the fennel over halfway. Transfer to a large bowl and season with the ground kelp. Set aside. Repeat with the remaining fennel.

In a separate bowl, combine the salt, sugar and shallot. Set aside for 10 minutes, then stir in the remaining 140 ml (4½ fl oz) oil and the vinegar. Add this dressing to the fennel and leave in a warm place.

For the bonito, using a sharp knife, split the loin from the belly by cutting down the lateral line of the fish. Cut the loin and belly into four even portions, weighing 90–100 g (3–3½ oz) each.

To poach the bonito, wrap a small saucer or plate in plastic wrap so that it's taut across the plate from edge to edge, then place in a large saucepan with the olive oil, peppercorns and herbs. Heat over a low heat until the oil reaches a temperature of 48°C (118°F). Add the loins, as they will take a little longer to cook than the belly, and leave them in the warm oil for 12–15 minutes. Once the loin is cooked, remove the pan from the heat and leave for a further 5 minutes, then remove the loin and leave to rest on a plate while the bellies are cooked in the same way. This time for 10 minutes as they are thinner.

To serve, place a spoonful of the dressing in the centre of a plate, place the bonito in the middle, season well and finish with a broken sheet of potato.

Native Australian Fish Curry

Fish curry is such an important dish in the global seafood repertoire. There are so many variations based on where it's cooked (be that Thailand, India or England) that I wanted to create a recipe using native Australian ingredients, such as pepperberry, native ginger, turmeric leaves and native thyme to produce a curry that was light and fragrant. I've reproduced that recipe here, but have also provided details for alternative herbs and spices that are more widely available.

SERVES 8

100 g (3½ oz/½ cup) raw
　(demerara) sugar
100 ml (3½ fl oz) Fish Garum
　(see page 73) or good-quality fish
　sauce, plus extra if necessary
6 litres (202 fl oz/24 cups)
　coconut water
8 Murray cod chops (best alternative is
　cutting the fish as darnes; see note)
juice of 2 limes

Pickled red grapes

975 ml (33 fl oz) red-wine vinegar
375 g (13 oz/1⅔ cups) caster
　(superfine) sugar
1 tablespoon salt
600 g (1 lb 5 oz) red grapes

Curry paste

2 tablespoons each coriander seeds,
　fennel seeds and black peppercorns
1 tablespoon ground sichuan pepper
600 g (1 lb 5 oz) French shallots
100 g (3½ oz) garlic cloves
100 g (3½ oz) peeled ginger
4 native turmeric leaves or 50 g (1¾ oz)
　fresh turmeric, roughly chopped
4 native ginger leaves or 50 g (1¾ oz)
　fresh ginger, roughly chopped
4 kaffir lime leaves
½ smoked eel, skin and bone intact,
　cut into 2 cm (¾ in) lengths
400 g (14 oz) salted chilli
　(see page 66) or mild chilli,
　seeds removed
3 native thyme or lemon thyme sprigs,
　leaves picked
750 ml (25½ fl oz/3 cups)
　grapeseed oil

ALTERNATIVE FISH:
Bass grouper
Hake
Turbot

To pickle the grapes, bring the vinegar, sugar and salt to the boil in a saucepan over a high heat. Pour the hot syrup over the grapes in a plastic container to completely cover. Place baking paper on top to keep the grapes submerged and chill for at least 2 hours, ideally overnight or longer. The grapes will keep in the pickle for months.

For the curry paste, toast all the seeds and peppercorns in separate batches in a frying pan over a medium heat until fragrant, then add half the spices and half the remaining paste ingredients to a food processor and blitz to a smooth paste. Repeat until all the spices are blended and the paste is well mixed.

Heat a wide, heavy-based saucepan over a medium–high heat for 5 minutes, add the curry paste and stir-fry for 15 minutes. The key here is to cook these ingredients thoroughly in the beginning to establish a well-balanced flavour in the final stock.

Add the sugar and garum and cook for 10 minutes to caramelise the sugar. Add the coconut water, then bring the stock to the boil, reduce the heat and cook gently for 45 minutes, or until the stock has reduced by half. Remove from the heat and leave to rest for at least 20 minutes.

Using a large ladle and coarse sieve, push the stock through the sieve, then divide the stock into a larger pot for poaching and a saucepan.

Bring the larger pot for poaching to the boil, then remove from the heat and place four of the chops in, cover with a lid and poach for 10 minutes off the heat. Gently reheat the stock in the medium pan, then taste and season with the lime juice and more garum, if necessary.

Once the fish is poached, carefully remove the chops being careful not to break the skin and leave to rest on a plate, then cook the rest of the fish in the same way.

Serve the fish with the warmed stock poured over and with a herb salad, brown rice, the pickled grapes and any other pickles of your choice.

Note: A darne, also known as a cutlet, is a bone-in steak cut from the lower half of the fish. Being from the lower half means that there is just one central bone, which is easy to eat around. It will also help the fish retain its shape while cooking as well as give you a more flavourful fish and stock.

See photo on following pages.

Saint Peter's Fish Soup

This soup is in the style of a conventional bouillabaisse, but with some adjustments. Once the fundamentals of this soup are mastered it's a blank canvas for using ingredients that go beyond the parameters of this recipe (you can use native ingredients from the location you are in, for example, which can dramatically alter the flavour profile of what is a fairly universally known fish stew). Be patient when cooking this – the results will be better if care is taken in cooking the fish.

SERVES 6

Soup base

2.5 kg (5½ lb) small whole
　　leatherjackets or triggerfish
2.5 kg (5½ lb) whole red spot whiting
2.5 kg (5½ lb) small whole red mullet
2.5 kg (5½ lb whole red gurnard
2.5 kg (5½ lb) gutted bluespot
　　flathead or bream
120 ml (4 fl oz) extra-virgin olive oil
2.5 kg (5½ lb) small crab (blue
　　swimmer, brown or sand ideal)
shells and heads from 10 king prawns
　　(shrimp)
sea salt flakes and freshly ground
　　black pepper
3 onions, finely sliced
5 garlic cloves, crushed
1 fennel bulb, finely sliced
100 ml (3½ fl oz) tomato paste
　　(concentrated puree)
4 tomatoes, roughly chopped
½ bunch thyme sprigs
10 lemon thyme sprigs (optional)
1 teaspoon fennel seeds,
　　lightly toasted
1 star anise
4 dried ground bush tomato or use
　　a little smoked paprika (optional)
3 g (⅛ oz) saffron threads
lemon juice, to taste

For the soup base, using a sharp cleaver, chop the fish into small pieces. In a large, wide, heavy-based pot, heat 100 ml (3½ fl oz) olive oil and fry the crabs and prawn shells for 10–12 minutes until coloured. Set aside in a bowl.

Return the pot to a medium heat, and using the same oil, add the chopped fish. Season with a big pinch of salt and cook for 10 minutes until coloured all over. Set aside with the shellfish.

Using a wide barbecue scraper, scratch off the caramelised fish from the base of the pan and set aside with the fish. Add the remaining olive oil and heat over a medium heat. Sweat the onions for 10 minutes, then increase the heat to high, add the garlic and fennel and cook for a further 5 minutes. Add the tomato paste and fry for 5 minutes until fragrant. Add all the fish and shellfish along with the remaining ingredients, cover with water, place a lid on top and bring to the boil. As soon as it's boiling, uncover and cook over a high heat for 20 minutes.

Pass the stock through a mouli or pulse in a food processor, then strain and season well with salt, lemon juice and pepper.

Rouille

1 red capsicum (bell pepper),
  roasted and peeled
1 long red chilli, seeds removed
2 potatoes, peeled and diced
50 g (1¾ oz/1/3 cup) roasted
  macadamia nuts
5 garlic cloves
2 dried ground bush tomatoes
  (optional)
¼ teaspoon smoked paprika
pinch of saffron threads
210 ml (7 fl oz) extra-virgin olive oil

Finishing garnishes

500 g (1 lb 2 oz) small waxy potatoes,
  such as dutch cream or bintje,
  skin on
5 x 120 g (4½ oz) red mullet, gutted
  and scaled
200 g (7 oz) john dory roe
400 g (14 oz) cuttlefish or squid
  tentacles
500 g (1 lb 2 oz) pipis or clams,
  de-sanded
10 king prawns (shrimp), peeled
  and deveined
50 g (1¾ oz) ghee
250 g (9 oz) best available fish liver
  (e.g. john dory, grouper or cod)

To serve

1 good-quality rye loaf
100 g (3½ oz) cold good-quality
  salted cultured butter
250 g (9 oz) mixed herb salad leaves

For the rouille, place all the ingredients, except the olive oil, in a stainless-steel saucepan, pour in enough of the fish soup to cover and cook until the potatoes are very soft. Drain, reserving the liquid. Blend the potatoes in a food processor with 40 ml (1¼ fl oz) of the reserved liquid to a smooth puree, then gradually whisk in the olive oil. When the sauce is thick and silky season well with salt and a squeeze of lemon juice.

Divide the rest of the soup base between a large and a medium saucepan. Add the potatoes to the medium pan and cook for 15–20 minutes until tender, then set aside.

Bring the soup base in the large pan to the boil. Remove from the heat and add the mullet, john dory roe and tentacles. Cover and cook for 4–5 minutes. Set the fish aside on a plate.

Return the soup base to the boil, then remove from the heat, add the pipis and prawns and cook for 3 minutes. Take the pipis out when they open. Reserve the shellfish alongside the fish on a plate.

Heat the ghee in a frying pan over a high heat. Sauté the fish liver until golden brown on both sides, about 1 minute. Be careful not to overcook the liver.

To bring the whole dish together, build the cooked ingredients in a large bowl or dish. Bring the soup base that has poached all the seafood back to a simmer and pour a generous amount over the dish. Serve with bread, butter, a green salad, the rouille and a cold bottle(s) of chardonnay.

ALTERNATIVE FISH:
Gurnard
Mullet
Snapper

See photo on page 121.

Smoked Ocean Trout Rillette, Almonds & Radishes

I first made this rillette dish when I was working as a chef at Cafe Nice in Sydney – it was a way to use up the waste from the trout fillets we were cutting for use as a main course. My apprentice Ollie and I produced 600 portions of this dish as a canapé for an event in Shanghai the year before Saint Peter opened. Fair to say, we were both sick of it for a while after that.

SERVES 2

80 g (2¾ oz/¼ cup) fine salt
2 dill sprigs
1 teaspoon toasted fennel seeds
250 g (9 oz) skinless, boneless ocean trout or sea trout bellies, tail or trim
1 x 14 g (½ oz) applewood smoking puck
500 ml (17 fl oz/2 cups) grapeseed oil
3 tablespoons Garlic mayonnaise (see page 110)
1 teaspoon finely chopped tarragon
1 teaspoon finely chopped flat-leaf (Italian) parsley
1 teaspoon finely chopped chives
2 tablespoons toasted flaked almonds
juice of ½ lemon
sea salt flakes and freshly cracked black pepper
15 small red breakfast radishes

Blitz the salt, dill and fennel seeds together in a spice grinder, then rub this mix over the trout flesh and leave to cure for at least 4 hours, or ideally overnight.

The next day, rinse the fish under cold water and pat dry with paper towel.

Cold smoke the trout in a smoker for 20–30 minutes depending on your preferred degree of smokiness. Alternatively, line the top of a cheap double steamer with foil, add soaked wood chips to the base and use this to cold smoke the fish.

Heat the oil in a saucepan until the oil reaches a temperature of 48°C (118°F). Place the smoked trout in the pan and leave in the warm oil for 12–15 minutes until set through. The fish should be just cooked. Drain the fish on paper towel, then transfer to a bowl. Cover and leave to cool in the refrigerator.

Use a fork to shred the cooled fish into a coarse texture similar to a meat rillette. Add the mayonnaise, herbs and toasted almonds and season with lemon juice, salt and pepper.

Using a sharp mandoline, slice the radishes into thin even discs. Set aside.

To assemble the rillette, use a large kitchen spoon to scoop a mound of the trout mix into the centre of the plate making an egg shape and assemble the radishe slices over the top to resemble fish scales as pictured. I enjoy eating this dish with raw witlof (endive/chicory) leaves or toasted sourdough.

ALTERNATIVE FISH:
Arctic char
Spanish mackerel
Trout

Head Terrine, Mustard & Pickles

I love this style of cooking, where simple ingredients that are well looked after and thoughtfully prepared can be translated into a show-stopping dish. Once you've got over the 'fish head' mental hurdle, this will be a recipe you come back to again and again. It is imperative that the cooked fish head is thoroughly picked over before pressing into the terrine.

SERVES 12

5 litres (160 fl oz/20 cups) Brown Fish Stock (see page 67), plus an extra 500 ml (17 fl oz/2 cups) reduced to 300 ml (10 fl oz) for setting terrine
6 coral trout heads or other fish heads of a similar weight, about 500 g (1 lb 2 oz) each (e.g. wild kingfish, red snapper, sea bass, hapuka or flametail snapper)
1 bunch chives, finely sliced
1 bunch chervil leaves, finely sliced
½ bunch flat-leaf (Italian) parsley, finely sliced
4 French shallots, finely diced
60 g (2 oz/½ cup) capers
60 g (2 oz/⅓ cup) gherkins or cornichons, finely diced
2 teaspoons dijon mustard
sea salt flakes and freshly cracked black pepper

Bring the 5 litres (160 fl oz/20 cups) fish stock to the boil in a large stockpot. Remove from the heat, submerge two of the heads under the hot stock and cover with a lid. Cook for about 12–15 minutes until the flesh from the head slips off evenly. Repeat the process three times until all six heads are cooked.

Once cooked and while the heads are still hot, wearing disposable gloves, begin to pick the flesh from the head making sure to avoid any scales, bone or cartilage. Once all the flesh has been picked, pick over one more time.

Once the fish is cool but not completely cold, add all the herbs, shallots, capers, gherkins or cornichons, mustard and the 300 ml (10 fl oz) reduced stock. Season to taste, then either roll the mixture into a log or place it in a 1 kg (2 lb 3 oz) terrine mould lined with plastic wrap. If doing the latter, pack the mix in tightly with no gaps or air pockets (you can also add different garnishes to the terrine, such as soft-boiled eggs or vegetables). Leave it to set in the refrigerator overnight.

Serve with a herb salad, good mustard, homemade pickles, cold butter and hot rye bread.

ALTERNATIVE FISH:
Grouper
Hake
Hapuka

Fish Cassoulet

Once we had developed our recipes for fish sausages and bacon, I felt it was time we produced a dish in the style of a cassoulet. Yet it was only when Fish Butchery opened that we finally made it happen. When making this dish, break it down into smaller tasks and plan ahead, otherwise it can feel a little overwhelming. I wanted to include this recipe here as it was one of the first dishes I began thinking about in relation to the ways that meat cookery can merge into the fish world.

SERVES 4

100 g (3½ oz/½ cup) dried cannellini (lima) beans
1 smoked eel, cut into 4 cm (1½ in) lengths
120 g (4½ oz) ghee
1 carrot, finely chopped
1 onion, finely diced
12 thyme sprigs
1 garlic bulb
1 tomato, finely chopped
1.5 litres (51 fl oz/6 cups) Brown Fish Stock (see page 67)
1 × 200 g (7 oz) piece smoked Swordfish Bacon (see page 60), cut into thick batons
4 Fish Sausages (see page 206)
600 g (1 lb 5 oz) Spanish mackerel darnes (see note, page 115), pin-boned and sliced into 4 steaks
1 × 400 g (14 oz) brioche loaf
1 smoked Spanish mackerel heart
1 tablespoon diced tarragon leaves
½ teaspoon sea salt

Soak the cannellini beans in cold water overnight.

To prepare the smoked eel, peel the outer black skin off and set aside. Using a small knife, fillet the flesh off the bone. Set the bones and flesh aside.

Heat 60 g (2 oz/¼ cup) of the ghee in a wide, heavy-based saucepan over a high heat and cook the carrot and onion for 5 minutes, or until slightly coloured and softened. Add the reserved smoked eel skin and bones and fry for a further 5 minutes. Add the thyme, garlic and tomato and cover with the fish stock. Bring to the boil, reduce the heat and simmer for 15–20 minutes until slightly thickened. Remove from the heat and leave to infuse while cooling.

Once cool, pass the stock into a clean, large saucepan. Add the soaked beans and bring to the boil. Reduce the heat and simmer for 45 minutes–1 hour, or until tender.

In a frying pan, fry the bacon in the remaining ghee for 6–7 minutes until the bacon is dark and well caramelised. Set aside.

Fry the sausages in the same pan for 4 minutes, or until golden on all sides. Set aside with the bacon.

Deglaze the hot pan that was used to cook the bacon and sausages with two ladles of the hot stock. Scratch off the particles on the bottom of the pan and add to the stock. Bring the stock to the boil over a medium heat, then remove from the heat and add the mackerel steaks. Cover and cook off the heat for 5 minutes. Remove the fish with a slotted spoon and transfer to a plate. The fish at this stage should only be 60 per cent cooked.

Remove the crusts from the brioche and blitz in a food processor to coarse breadcrumbs. Microplane the mackerel heart into the breadcrumbs and add the tarragon. Season with the salt and set aside.

Preheat the oven grill. Arrange the mackerel steaks in a large casserole or heatproof serving dish, along with the bacon, sausages, the eel fillets (which have been broken into small pieces), cooked beans and enough stock to go halfway up the ingredients. Sprinkle the breadcrumbs over to completely cover the top and grill for 8–10 minutes until the breadcrumbs are golden and the edge of the dish begins to bubble. Leave for 2–3 minutes before serving. Salt-roasted cabbage (see page 152) or celeriac would be a wonderful winter addition to this robust dish.

ALTERNATIVE FISH:
Blue-eye trevalla
Leatherjacket
Haddock

See photo overleaf.

FRIED
(DEEP, SHALLOW & PAN)

Great fish for fried fish
preparations include:

Bream

Gurnard

Halibut

Herring

John dory

Kingfish

Mackerel

Mahi-mahi

Meagre (Jewfish)

Mullet

Murray cod

Pilchards

Plaice

Sea bass

Sprats

Trumpeter

Whiting

Fried fish, what more needs to be said? Globally known, globally loved. Whether it's fried haddock and vinegared chips on a wharf in Cornwall or Southern-fried catfish and grits in Nashville, all these provoke a sense of nostalgia and comfort, hence why they are so loved.

I prefer to use ghee or clarified butter for pan- and shallow-frying instead of cooking oils as ghee has a high smoking point of 250°C (482°). The flavour is also superior to other oils, giving the fish skin a sweet characteristic only a derivative of butter could produce.

When shallow- and pan-frying I find that when the fish is turned to the flesh side when cooking for a prolonged period of time, too much damage is done to the flesh, resulting in dryness and a texture that's too firm. If the species has an edible skin it is always better left on.

When shallow- and pan-frying fish the choice of pan is really up to you. I pan-fry in thin cast-iron skillets as they generate a lot of heat very quickly. The following recipes are intended to help you understand how to be more confident when cooking with different fats and temperatures.

Left, overleaf & page 134: Coral trout (aged 3 days).

CRISP-SKIN FISH ESSENTIALS

There are a number of key points to bear in mind when pan-frying fish on the skin.

1.

THE FISH. Be sure the fish is ambient before adding to the hot pan. If cooking straight from the fridge, the protein will set unevenly and it will be challenging to determine doneness, especially as fish has a relatively short cooking time.

2.

THE FAT. To cook crisp-skin fish I use a small amount of ghee to begin the process, which I discard after 2 minutes of cooking and replenish with another small amount to finish the cooking.

3.

THE FISH WEIGHT. I would find it difficult, if not impossible, to pan-fry or grill fish well without this piece of kitchen equipment, which can be found easily enough online. These weights are not designed to be heated. When pan-frying a fish on the skin, the heat that's generated crisps the skin, which travels up through the muscle of the fish and sits on the face of the weight. This sets the top of the fillet very gently while forcing the skin to have direct contact with the pan. By using a weight on thin to thickish fillets, you will be able to cook the fish from raw to cooked on the stove and rely less on the oven to finish cooking, However, if cooking a very thick fillet, start by using the weight to crisp the skin, then once you see the first signs of colour, remove the weight and transfer to an oven to complete cooking. An alternative to a fish weight would be to use a small, heavy-based saucepan filled with water, though this will be considerably more fiddly.

4.

THE HEAT. The heat we use to cook with is a target top gas stove, which is one large square of intense heat. I don't enjoy cooking over gas burners as a very high heat is needed to cook crisp fish skin and the flames of a gas stove can often flare up during cooking when moisture spits from the pan. However, if you have a gas burner, don't tilt the pan too much when cooking fish as beads of moisture can hit the fat and cause flames to surround the fish. Constant, uninterrupted heat is key to creating a crisp, glassy skin and pearl-like flesh – temperature control is everything.

Fried Whitebait

This is a simple snack that we like having on the menu at Fish Butchery. It requires very little work, though I have suggested removing the fried whitebait from the fryer and finishing cooking over a charcoal grill as it adds a savoury smoky flavour to the fish and will help the small fish stay crisper for longer. Always check whitebait before serving to friends as they can carry sand in their gills and scales, which is unnoticeable to the eye.

SERVES 4

2 litres (68 fl oz/8 cups) canola (rapeseed) or grapeseed oil, for deep-frying
480 g (1 lb 1 oz) whitebait (sandy sprats), de-sanded
200 g (7 oz/1 cup) fine rice flour
sea salt flakes
1½ teaspoons ground black pepper
½ teaspoon ground sichuan pepper
⅛ teaspoon ground juniper berries

Heat the oil for deep-frying in a large saucepan over a medium–high heat until it reaches a temperature of 180°C (350°F).

If a charcoal barbecue is accessible or a small gas burning barbecue, then use this for the second part of the cooking. This is an optional additional method of cookery, but one that elevates the flavour of the whitebait. Light the barbecue.

Place half the whitebait in a coarse sieve and add enough rice flour to lightly coat. Shake the sieve to remove the excess flour, then repeat with the other half of the fish. Tip a small batch of the dusted whitebait carefully into the hot oil and deep-fry for 45 seconds. Remove and drain on paper towel. Season well with salt. Repeat until all the whitebait is fried, then arrange them on a wire rack. Position this rack over the hottest part of the grill and, using a spoon, toss the whitebait around so that the outside of the fish chars and colours evenly.

Transfer the fish to a bowl and season liberally with the pepper, sichuan pepper, ground juniper berries and more salt. Serve immediately as a snack before dinner or while enjoying drinks with mayonnaise or gentleman's relish and a lemon wedge.

ALTERNATIVE FISH:
Anchovies
Pilchards
Sprats

Fish & Chips

Quite possibly the most famous fish dish of them all, this is my interpretation of the simple yet challenging household favourite. I was introduced to this style of batter when I was a stagiaire at Heston Blumenthal's Fat Duck in Bray, England, and for me it is the best batter there is. I have chosen butterflied yellow-eye mullet for this recipe instead of a traditional fillet as the presentation is impressive, and the natural oils in the mullet keep the fish moist and flavourful. Note: if you want to cook the chips in this way, this recipe needs to be started 4 days ahead.

SERVES 4

3 kg (6 lb 10 oz) potatoes, such as sebago, king edward or russet burbank, skin on
salt
5 litres (160 fl oz/20 cups) cottonseed or sunflower oil, for deep-frying
4 skinless, boneless butterflied yellow-eye mullet, ling, haddock or pollock fillets, head and tail on
215 g (7½ oz/1½ cups) self-raising flour
400 g (14 oz/2¼ cups) rice flour, plus extra for dusting
2 teaspoons baking powder
2 tablespoons honey
345 ml (11½ fl oz) vodka (37% proof)
550 ml (18½ fl oz) beer

For the potato chips, cut the potatoes into index finger width and length batons, then soak in cold water overnight.

The next day, drain the chips and transfer them to a large, heavy-based stock pot. Cover with cold water and season with salt. Bring to the boil and cook for 10 minutes, or until the potatoes are moments from collapsing but still holding their form. Remove the potatoes carefully and transfer to wire racks. Leave to dry in the freezer overnight, uncovered.

The next day, heat the oil for deep-frying in a deep-fryer or large saucepan until it reaches a temperature of 140°C (284°F). Deep-fry the chips for 5 minutes, or until a blistered skin on the chip has fully formed. Drain and leave to cool, then return to the freezer to dry on a wire rack overnight.

The next day, prepare the fish by slicing even thick medallions from the fillet and setting on paper towel in readiness to flour and batter.

For the batter, whisk the flours and baking powder together in a large bowl. Mix the honey and vodka together well, then pour into the flour mix. Add the beer and whisk together. Chill until needed.

Heat the frying oil in the saucepan to 180°C (350°F) and fry the parcooked chips again until very crisp and golden, about 5–6 minutes. Drain well and season with salt.

Dust the fish lightly in a little rice flour first, then coat in the batter and carefully lower into the hot oil. Deep-fry for 2 minutes, or until very crisp. You may need to turn the fish over midway through for even colouring. Remove and drain on a wire rack set in a tray.

Serve the fish and chips immediately with your favourite condiments, a green salad and cold beer (or kombucha).

ALTERNATIVE FISH:
Gurnard
Haddock
Ling

See photo on following pages.

Buttermilk Fried Blue-Eye Trevalla

Given the massive popularity of buttermilk-marinated fried chicken, I thought we could try out something similar with fish. Through trial and error we have landed on this recipe, which provides a wonderfully crisp, light coating on the exterior and silky, juicy flesh on the interior. Blue-eye trevalla is a brilliant fish for this style of preparation as its flesh is very juicy, though large john dory, cod or grouper would all work well. It's best enjoyed with a cold beer or between slices of white bread with a good coleslaw.

SERVES 6

1 kg (2 lb 3 oz/3⅓ cups) blue-eye trevalla bone-in chops, skin on (or use john dory, cod, grouper, gurnard, turbot or flounder)
500 g (1 lb 2 oz) tapioca starch
canola (rapeseed) or cottonseed oil, for deep-frying

Seasoning mix

50 g (1¾ oz) ground sumac
50 g (1¾ oz) smoked paprika
50 g (1¾ oz) freshly ground black pepper
50 g (1¾ oz) freshly ground coriander seed
200 g (7 oz/¾ cup) fine sea salt

Marinade

300 ml (10 fl oz) buttermilk
500 ml (17 fl oz/2 cups) Kewpie mayonnaise (Japanese mayonnaise)
1 tablespoon dijon mustard
80 ml (2½ oz/⅓ cup) white-wine vinegar

For the seasoning mix, combine all the ingredients in a bowl and store in an airtight container until required.

Combine all the marinade ingredients in a large bowl. Arrange the fish chops on a baking tray, then tip the marinade over the fish. Wearing disposable gloves, rub the marinade over the fish, making sure the fish is well coated. Leave, uncovered, in the refrigerator for 4–6 hours.

Coat the fish in the tapioca starch until it looks like a coarse batter around the fish, then leave, uncovered, in the refrigerator overnight.

The next day, remove the fish from the refrigerator at least 1 hour before frying. Heat the oil for deep-frying in a deep-fryer or a large, heavy-based saucepan to a temperature of 190°C (375°F) and fry the fish for 4–5 minutes until the internal temperature is 58°C (136°F). Remove and drain on a wire rack set inside a baking tray for 4 minutes.

Season the fish thoroughly with the seasoning mix and serve with lemon or your favourite condiments.

ALTERNATIVE FISH:
Hake
Mahi-mahi
Sea bass

Crumbed Garfish, Yoghurt Tartare & Herb Salad

I absolutely love crumbed fish (I think it's partly due to growing up eating fish fingers and mashed potato as a kid). I love, too, that crumbed fish needn't be limited to fillets of unknown white fish but can be as luxurious as this boneless, butterflied garfish. Don't cut corners when it comes to how you cook it, though – always in a hot frying pan with ghee, not deep-fried!

SERVES 4

4 x 200 g (7 oz) garfish, scaled, gutted, gilled and reverse butterflied (see page 55)
150 g (5½ oz/1 cup) plain (all-purpose) flour
4 eggs, lightly whisked
120 g (4½ oz/2 cups) white panko breadcrumbs
400 g (14 oz) ghee
sea salt flakes and freshly cracked white/black pepper
lemon wedges

Yoghurt tartare sauce

375 g (13 oz/1½ cups) natural yoghurt
3 large French shallots, diced
1 tablespoon small salted capers, rinsed, dried and finely chopped
60 g (2 oz/⅓ cup) coarsely chopped cornichons
2 tablespoons finely sliced flat-leaf (Italian) parsley leaves

Herb salad

pinch of salt
1 teaspoon caster (superfine) sugar
6 French shallots, finely sliced into rings
140 ml (4½ fl oz) extra-virgin olive oil
50 ml (1¾ fl oz) chardonnay vinegar or white-wine vinegar with a pinch of sugar
1 bunch each of flat-leaf (Italian) parsley, dill, chervil and French tarragon, leaves picked
30 g (1 oz/1 cup) watercress leaves
35 g (1¼ oz/1 cup) wild rocket (arugula) leaves
2 large butter lettuce, broken into bite-sized pieces

ALTERNATIVE FISH:
Herring
Mullet
Whiting

For the sauce, stir all the ingredients together in a bowl. Set aside.

Preheat the oven to 100°C (210°F).

Holding the fish by the tail, dip one fish into the flour, then in the egg, then in the breadcrumbs, pressing gently to coat it well. Place on a baking tray and repeat with the remaining fish.

Heat one-third of the ghee in a large frying pan over a high heat. When hot, fry two fish for 2 minutes, or until crisp and golden, then turn and cook the other side for a further minute. Place on a baking tray and keep warm in the oven. Wipe the pan, then repeat with the remaining ghee and fish.

For the herb salad, combine the salt, sugar and shallot in a bowl. Leave for 10 minutes, then stir in the olive oil and vinegar. Combine the herbs, watercress, rocket and lettuce in a separate bowl, then toss with enough of the dressing to lightly coat the leaves (any leftover dressing will keep refrigerated in an airtight container for up to a week).

Season the fish liberally and serve with lemon wedges, generous spoonfuls of the sauce and the herb salad on the side.

Crumbed Sardine Sandwich

Who doesn't love a crumbed fish sandwich on soft white bread? It's important to fry the sardines in ghee in a pan rather then deep-frying, as the flavour is much better and the degree of cooking is easier to control. Yoghurt tartare sauce (see page 144) could be substituted for a hot sauce or mayonnaise, if you like. This sandwich is so versatile and a number of different fish work perfectly here, including herring, whiting, bream or flathead.

SERVES 2

150 g (5½ oz/1 cup) plain
    (all-purpose) flour
4 eggs, lightly whisked
120 g (4½ oz/2 cups) white panko
    breadcrumbs
8 x 60 g (2 oz) sardines, scaled,
    gutted and butterflied
70 g (2½ oz) ghee
sea salt flakes and freshly cracked
    black pepper
4 slices soft white bread
100 g (3½ oz) Yoghurt tartare sauce
    (see page 144)

Start by flouring, egg washing and crumbing the butterflied sardines, being sure to leave the tails of the fish uncrumbed.

Heat the ghee in a frying pan over a high heat and cook the crumbed sardines, in batches, on one side for 1 minute, or until golden and crisp, then flip to the other side and fry for a further 10–20 seconds. Remove from the pan and season liberally.

Cut the crusts off the bread. Spread some of the sauce over two of the slices of bread from edge to edge, then arrange four sardines on top. Add the remaining sauce on top and then the remaining slices of bread.

Serve with the golden edges of the sardine showing around the edges of the bread and the little tails exposed at one end.

ALTERNATIVE FISH:
Anchovies
Herring
Whiting

Fish Collar Cutlet

From species to species, it never ceases to surprise me just how much flesh can be found in the collar of a fish. I've suggested serving these here with a fennel mayonnaise – and a herb salad or some pickles would make good accompaniments – but really any garnish that would traditionally be paired with a pork or chicken cutlet would work perfectly with this dish.

SERVES 4

4 red emperor collars
2 tablespoons fennel seeds
120 g (4½ oz/2 cups) white panko
 breadcrumbs
150 g (5½ oz/1 cup) plain
 (all-purpose) flour
4 eggs, beaten
80 g (2¾ oz) ghee
sea salt flakes and freshly cracked
 black pepper

Wild fennel mayonnaise (optional)

2 egg yolks
½ tablespoon dijon mustard
2 teaspoons white-wine vinegar
fine salt, to taste
250 ml (8½ fl oz/1 cup) grapeseed oil
juice of ½ lemon, to taste
1 tablespoon fennel pollen, celery
 seeds or ground fennel, to taste

For the mayonnaise, rest a bowl on a tea towel (dish towel) draped over a saucepan to stabilise it. Add the egg yolks, mustard, vinegar and salt to the bowl and whisk together well. Continue whisking, slowly drizzle in the oil to form a thick emulsion. Taste and add salt, lemon juice and fennel pollen to taste. It should be the thickness of softly whipped cream, so adjust with a little warm water if necessary.

Place the fish collars, skin side down, on a chopping board. Using a short, sharp knife, cut the bones out of the collar. This is done by using your fingers to feel the outline of the bone, then getting the blade as close to the bone while cutting to take it out. Using a coarse meat mallet, lightly tap the collar out into the shape of a cutlet or 'pork chop'.

Add the fennel seeds to the panko breadcrumbs. Dust the collar with flour, then coat in the egg and the breadcrumbs. Make sure to keep the collar wing uncrumbed.

Heat a frying pan over a high heat, add the ghee and wait until there is a light haze. Shallow-fry two collar cutlets at a time for 1½ minutes on each side until golden. Drain on paper towel, then season well.

Leave the cutlets whole or slice into pieces and serve with the wild fennel mayonnaise or lemon halves for squeezing.

ALTERNATIVE FISH:
Bream
Red snapper

Jackass Morwong, Salt Roast Sugarloaf Cabbage & Nettle Sauce

The first time I ate this deep sea bream I couldn't believe how good it was. To me it resembled one of Australia's finest fish, striped trumpeter, both in texture and flavour. Good-quality line-caught fish will have a nice layer of fat under the skin and will perform so well in a pan or on a grill. Enjoy this dish in the cooler months when the nettles and cabbages are juicy and the fish is fatty.

SERVES 4

4 x 175 g (6 oz) boneless jackass
    morwong, skin on
200 g (7 oz) ghee
sea salt flakes

Salt roast cabbage

300 g (10½ oz/2 cups) plain
    (all-purpose) flour, plus extra
    for dusting
210 g (7½ oz/¾ cup) fine salt
75 g (2¾ oz) egg whites
150 ml (5 fl oz) water
1 large whole sugarloaf (hispi/savoy)
    cabbage
lemon juice, to taste

Nettle sauce

1 litre (34 fl oz/4 cups) water
100 g (3½ oz/⅓ cup) fine salt
400 g (14 oz) stinging nettle leaves
1 tablespoon cornichon or caper brine
    (store bought is fine)
3 anchovy fillets
100 g (3½ oz) cold butter, cubed
sea salt flakes and freshly cracked
    black pepper
2 tablespoons natural yoghurt

ALTERNATIVE FISH:
Bream
Red snapper

If there is any surface moisture on the fish, arrange the fish on a wire rack, skin side up, and leave to chill for at least 2 hours before pan-frying.

If a charcoal barbecue is accessible or small gas burning barbecue, then use this for the second part of the cooking. Light the barbecue.

For the roast cabbage, preheat the oven to 180°C (350°F).

Using a stand mixer fitted with a dough hook attachment, mix the flour, salt, egg whites and water on low speed for 5 minutes, or until a firm dough forms. Turn the dough out onto a lightly floured surface and knead into a ball. Cover with plastic wrap and rest for at least 1 hour.

Rinse the cabbage briefly, then uncover the salt dough and roll out to a thickness of 3 mm (⅛ in). Drape the pastry over the cabbage and wrap completely, enclosing the cabbage. Bake the cabbage on a baking tray lined with baking paper for 6 hours, or until very soft and the pastry is a dark caramel colour. Leave the cabbage to rest for at least 20 minutes before breaking into it.

For the sauce, bring the water and salt to the boil in a large lidded pot. Add the nettles and stir to submerge them fully. Cover and cook for 30 seconds, then remove and wring out all the moisture between clean tea towels (dish towels).

Have a bowl filled with iced water ready. Blitz the caper brine, anchovy and nettles in a blender for 1 minute, or until a puree forms. Begin adding cubes of butter to the puree until emulsified and the sauce is viscous and shiny. Pour the nettle puree into a bowl and sit in the bowl of iced water. Stir until completely chilled. Leave in the fridge until needed. As there is the brine from the capers, after a few hours the sauce will begin to discolour from the acid. Alternatively, use the caper brine as a seasoning at the last minute.

To cook the fish, heat a cast-iron skillet or frying pan over a high heat. Add 60 g (2 oz/¼ cup) of the ghee and wait until there is a light haze. Add two fillets, making sure they are not touching, and position a fish weight on a top of the thickest side of the fillets. When you see colour around the edges of the fillet, about 1 minute, reposition the fillets in another part of the pan. Position the weight in the centre of the pan covering most of the fillets. After another minute, remove the weight, discard the ghee in the pan and replenish with 40 g (1½ oz) fresh ghee. If the fillet is cool to the touch, position the weight on top for 1–2 minutes. Once the fish is 75 per cent of the way set, the top of the fillet is warm and the skin is crisp, remove to a wire rack, skin side down.

This step isn't necessary but it makes the skin crisp. Position the fillets, skin side down, over a moderately hot part of the grill and, using a pair of small tongs, keep checking the skin is taking on colour.

Warm the nettle sauce, then season and spoon into the centre of warm serving plates. Spoon some yoghurt inside the sauce. Crack the crust of the cabbage with the back of a spoon and scoop the flesh out onto the plate, then add the fish. Season the fish skin liberally with salt. Serve immediately.

See photo on previous page.

Coral Trout & its Head, Rolled Silverbeet & Green Goddess

Coral trout is one of the finest eating fish in Australia and it is used here to showcase a number of different cuts and degrees of cooking. Amberjack, samson and mahi-mahi are all great alternate species to consider for this preparation.

SERVES 2

2 x 150 g (5½ oz) boneless coral
    trout fillets, skin on
100 g (3½ oz) ghee
2 x coral trout jowls
sea salt flakes
juice of ¼ lemon

Green goddess

1 litre (34 fl oz/4 cups) water
100 g (3½ oz) fine salt
100 g (3½ oz) flat-leaf (Italian)
    parsley leaves
50 g (1¾ oz) tarragon leaves
50 g (1¾ oz) dill leaves
1 bunch chives
50 ml (1¾ fl oz) caper brine
3 anchovy fillets
100 g (3½ oz) sour cream
sea salt flakes
pinch of caster (superfine) sugar

Rolled silverbeet

2 x coral trout collars
40 g (1½ oz) ghee
1 x coral trout throat, glazed in
    Verjuice dressing (see page 90)
sea salt flakes and freshly cracked
    black pepper
1 bunch silverbeet (Swiss chard)
    leaves, stems removed
juice of ¼ lemon
1 tablespoon finely chopped chives

For the green goddess, bring the water and salt to a rapid boil in a large pot. Add the herbs, stir to submerge them, then cover and cook for 30 seconds. Remove the herbs and wring out all of the moisture between clean tea towels (dish towels).

Have a bowl filled with iced water ready. Blitz the caper brine, anchovies and herbs to a puree in a blender for 2 minutes. Transfer to a bowl and sit in the bowl of iced water, stirring until chilled. Return the puree to the blender and blend in the sour cream. Season well with salt and the sugar and chill. As there is the brine from the capers, after a few hours the sauce will begin to discolour from the acid. Alternatively, use the caper brine as a seasoning at the last minute.

If a charcoal barbecue is accessible or small gas burning barbecue, then use this for the second part of the cooking. Light the barbecue.

Brush the collars with a little ghee and season with salt. Grill for 5 minutes, or until the flesh is translucent and the skin is bubbled. Leave to rest, then when cool enough to handle, pull the flesh from the cartilage and bone and add this to the fish throat. Set aside.

To cook the fillets, heat a cast-iron skillet or frying pan over a high heat. Add 60 g (2 oz/¼ cup) of the ghee and wait until there is a light haze. Add the fillets, making sure they are not touching one another and position a fish weight on top of the thickest side of the fillets. When you see colour around the edges of the fillet, about 2 minutes, reposition the fillets in another part of the pan. Position the weight in the centre of the pan covering most of the fillets. After 1 minute, remove the weight, discard the ghee and replenish with 40 g (1½ oz) of fresh ghee. If the fillet still seems cool to touch, position the weight on top for a further 3–4 minutes depending on the thickness. Once the fish is 75 per cent of the way set, the top of the fillet is warm and the skin is crisp, remove to a wire rack, skin side down.

This step isn't necessary but it makes the skin crisp. Position the crisp-skin fillets, skin side down, over a moderately hot part of the grill and, using a pair of small tongs, keep checking the skin is taking on colour.

Brush the trout jowls with ghee and season with salt. Grill over a medium heat until cooked through. The flesh should still remain translucent. Season with salt and lemon juice.

For the silverbeet, using the same pan that the trout was cooked in, melt the ghee, then lay the leaves down in strips on the bottom of the pan. Place a fish weight on top and cook for 2 minutes. Remove the weight and add the throat and collar pieces and roll up. Season with salt, pepper and a little lemon juice.

To serve, spoon 2 tablespoons of the green goddess into the centre of the plate, then place the fillet on top. Add the silverbeet rolls with the grilled jowls, then sprinkle a spoonful of chives on top of the silverbeet rolls and season.

ALTERNATIVE FISH:
Amberjack
Mahi-mahi
Samson

See photo on page 155.

Spanish Mackerel & Eggplant Offal XO

The eggplant here is nearly a dish on its own, with the offal XO adding so much umami and contrast to its silky, luxurious texture. Spanish mackerel at its very best will stand up brilliantly to the richness of the eggplant as it carries a wonderful natural acidity that has a citrus quality to it. Keep the Spanish mackerel underdone to no further than medium to experience the true texture and flavour of this delicious fish.

SERVES 4

2 medium eggplants (aubergines)
100 ml (3½ fl oz) extra-virgin olive oil
sea salt flakes and freshly cracked
    black pepper
200 g (7 oz) Offal XO Sauce
    (page 66)
100 g (3½ oz) ghee
2 x 300 g (10½ oz) Spanish
    mackerel fillets
200 g (7 oz/4 cups) baby English
    spinach or saltbush leaves
juice of 1 lime

To cook the eggplant, preheat the oven to 200°C (400°F) and line a baking tray with baking paper.

Peel the skin of the eggplants off and discard, then cut the eggplant into two even planks, 2.5–3 cm (1–1¼ in) thick. Brush them with the olive oil, season very lightly with salt and arrange the eggplant on the prepared baking tray. Place another square of baking paper on top of the eggplant and bake for 12–15 minutes until the eggplant is tender. Cool completely.

Spoon 50 g (1¾ oz) of XO sauce over each plank of eggplant, then grill the eggplant under a salamander grill or oven grill to develop a crust. Keep warm.

To cook the mackerel, heat a cast-iron skillet or frying pan over a high heat. Add 60 g (2 oz/¼ cup) of the ghee and wait until there is a light haze. Add the fillets, making sure they are not touching one another and position a fish weight on top of the thickest side. When you see colour around the edges of the fillet, about 1 minute, reposition the fillets in another part of the pan. Position the weight in the centre of the pan covering most of the fillets. After 3 more minutes remove the weight, discard the ghee and replenish with 40 g (1½ oz) of fresh ghee. If the fillet still seems cool to the touch, position the weight on top for a further 2 minutes depending on the thickness. Once the fish is 75 per cent of the way set, the top of the fillet is warm and the skin is crisp, remove from the heat, turn the fish over for 10 seconds, then transfer to a plate to rest.

Add the spinach to the pan and wilt while tossing with a spoon to coat in the ghee. Season with a little salt, black pepper and lime juice.

Place the fillet, skin side down, on a chopping board and, using a sharp knife, cut the fillet in half. Place one half in the centre of each plate. Fold the eggplant in half from top to bottom and position alongside the mackerel. Bury the spinach in and around the fish and eggplant. Add lime juice to the residual XO sauce on the baking tray and drizzle it over the eggplant. Season the mackerel with sea salt before serving.

ALTERNATIVE FISH:
Bugfish
Mackerel
Mahi-mahi

Striped Trumpeter, Pine Mushrooms, Parsley & Garlic

Striped trumpeter is in my top three eating fish in the world as it is the perfect balance of sweet and savoury. Because of this, you can push it in a sweet direction in terms of garnish choice, for example, through the use of peas, fennel or aromatic leaves and herbs. Alternatively, you can take it the other way and use more earthy savoury ingredients, such as salsify, artichokes, beetroot or indeed mushrooms, as in this dish here.

SERVES 4

200 g (7 oz) garlic cloves
50 g (1¾ oz/¼ cup) caster (superfine) sugar
150 g (5½ oz) salted butter
½ teaspoon native thyme or lemon thyme leaves
150 ml (5 fl oz) water
220 g (8 oz) ghee
300 g (10½ oz) pine mushrooms, chanterelles or field mushrooms, gills scraped out and cut into thick slices
100 ml (3½ fl oz) Brown Fish Stock (see page 67)
sea salt flakes and freshly cracked black pepper
juice of ½ lemon
1 bunch flat-leaf (Italian) parsley, leaves picked
4 x 180 g (6½ oz) boneless striped trumpeter, cod, bream, snapper or gurnard fillets, skin on

Preheat the oven to 200°C (400°F). Bring the garlic, sugar, 50 g (1¾ oz) of the butter, the thyme and water to the boil in an ovenproof frying pan and boil for 4 minutes. Transfer to the oven and cook for 10 minutes until all the liquid has evaporated, the garlic is tender and it is starting to take on colour. Return the pan to the stove and cook over a medium heat for a further 5 minutes. The garlic should be soft, sticky and sweet. Set aside.

Heat 120 g (4½ oz/½ cup) of the ghee in a large frying pan over a high heat. Add the mushrooms, season lightly with salt and sauté for 2 minutes until coloured and beginning to soften. Add your desired amount of caramelised garlic, the stock and the remaining butter, bring to a simmer and cook for 3–4 minutes, or until the liquid has reduced down to a thick glaze. Taste and adjust with more salt, lemon juice, parsley and pepper and cook for 30 seconds. Spoon the mushrooms and sauce onto four warmed serving plates and keep warm.

To cook the fish, heat a cast-iron skillet or frying pan over a high heat. Add 60 g (2 oz/¼ cup) of the ghee and wait until there is a light haze. Add two fillets, making sure they are not touching one another and position a fish weight on top of the thickest side of the fillets. When you see colour around the edges of the fillet, about 1 minute, reposition the fillets in another part of the pan. Position the weight in the centre of the pan covering most of the fillets. After 3 more minutes, remove the weight, discard the ghee and replenish with 40 g (1½ oz) of fresh ghee. If the fillets still seem cool to the touch, position the weight on top for a further 1–2 minutes depending on the thickness. Once the fish is 75 per cent of the way set, the top of the fillets are warm and the skin is crisp, arrange on top of the hot mushrooms. Cook the remaining fillets. Season the fish skin with sea salt and serve.

ALTERNATIVE FISH:
Hake
John dory
Turbot

John Dory Liver Pâté

A pâté is a preparation that I always wanted to apply to fish livers. In the height of winter, livers are in abundant supply from the well-fed fish they are cut from. Make sure you are meticulous with hygiene throughout the handling and cooking of the offal. Not all liver is good for this pâté, so look out for very firm fat livers from bar cod, john and mirror dory and wild kingfish when in season. This is delicious served with brioche toast and a good fruit chutney.

SERVES 4

2½ tablespoons white-wine vinegar
2½ tablespoons white wine
6 French shallots, finely sliced
½ teaspoon thyme leaves
2½ tablespoons ghee
300 g (10½ oz) john dory livers, trimmed
120 g (4½ oz) softened butter
sea salt flakes and freshly cracked black pepper

Heat the vinegar, wine, shallots and thyme in a small pan over a medium heat for 5 minutes, or until it has reduced to a syrup.

Heat the ghee in a frying pan over a high heat and wait until there is a haze over the pan. Sauté the livers until well caramelised on each side, about 1 minute in total. Transfer the livers to a blender along with the herb reduction and blend for 2 minutes, or until smooth.

Have a bowl filled with iced water ready. Remove the mixture from the blender and, using a pastry card or scraper, force this mixture through a drum or fine-mesh sieve into another bowl. Set the bowl over the iced water to cool slightly.

Whisk the butter in a stand mixer fitted with a whisk attachment until very pale and doubled in volume. Alternatively, use an electric whisk. Add the cool pâté to this butter and whisk for 2 minutes until smooth. Season well and chill for 1 hour before serving.

ALTERNATIVE FISH:
Blue-eye trevalla
Hake
Monkfish

Bar Cod Liver & Parsley on Toast

This is my favourite dish to cook, eat and serve to guests. The minerality and freshness of the barely cooked parsley nestled under the briefly seared cod liver to me is a wonderful way of celebrating an item totally undervalued by most.

SERVES 1

90 g (3 oz) ghee
200 g (7 oz) bar cod liver
1 tablespoon rice flour
30 g (1 oz) flat-leaf (Italian)
    parsley leaves
sea salt flakes and freshly cracked
    black pepper
juice of ¼ lemon
2 white sourdough bread slices
    about 1 cm (½ in) thick

Heat 30 g (1 oz) of the ghee in a cast-iron skillet or frying pan over a high heat.

Dust the liver with the flour and pat off the excess. Pan-fry the liver for 2½–3 minutes, depending on the thickness. The liver should have a golden brown exterior and blushing pink interior. Remove from the pan and, using the same pan and residual ghee, add the parsley and toss quickly, seasoning with salt and a squeeze of lemon juice for 15 seconds. Pour over the resting liver.

Heat a further 60 g (2 oz) of ghee in the pan and add the bread. Place a fish weight on top and cook for 1 minute, or until golden. Remove the weight, flip to the other side and cook for 30 seconds. Place next to the liver and parsley.

To assemble, carve the liver into four generous slices. Add the cooked parsley and season the toast.

ALTERNATIVE FISH:
Hake
John dory
Monkfish

Swordfish Bacon & Egg English Muffin

This muffin is a frequent item on the Saint Peter weekend lunch menu. If you didn't know what you were eating I believe it would go toe to toe with a pig-based bacon and egg muffin. Interpretations of this muffin with our fish sausage are also excellent, while the smoked eel hash brown on page 167 is also a killer addition to eat with this new brunch favourite.

SERVES 4

60 g (2 oz) ghee
200 g (7 oz) finely sliced smoked
    Swordfish Bacon (see page 60)
4 eggs
tomato sauce (ketchup)
freshly cracked black pepper

Muffins

500 g (1 lb 2 oz/3⅓ cups) baker's
    or strong bread flour
8 g (⅓ oz) salt
300 ml (10 fl oz) milk
1 whole egg
30 g (1 oz) soft butter
6 g (just under 2 teaspoons)
    fast-action dried yeast
plain (all-purpose) flour, for dusting
fine semolina, for dusting
120 g (4½ oz) ghee, for cooking

For the muffins, combine all the ingredients except the plain flour, fine semolina and ghee in a stand mixer fitted with a dough hook attachment and mix on low–medium speed for about 10 minutes. Transfer the dough to a lightly floured work surface and roll into a ball. Place the ball in an oiled bowl, cover with plastic wrap and leave to rise in the fridge overnight until doubled in size.

The next day, roll the dough out on a work surface dusted with semolina to a thickness of 1.5 cm (½ in). Using a conventional egg ring, cut out circles. Cover and leave to prove on the work surface for 10–15 minutes.

Preheat the oven to 150°C (300°F). Heat a frying pan, add a little of ghee and cook the muffins, in batches and adding more ghee as you go, for 2 minutes until they are a nice colour on both sides. Transfer to the oven and cook for a further 10 minutes, or until done.

Increase the oven temperature to 180°C (350°F). Heat half the ghee in an ovenproof frying pan over a high heat and fry the bacon for 4 minutes, or until crisp and golden. Remove and keep warm.

In the same pan, add the remaining ghee and fry the eggs inside four egg rings for 1 minute, or until the base of the egg is golden and crisp. Transfer to the oven for 1 minute.

Spoon some tomato sauce on a toasted muffin base then top with a generous amount of crisp bacon followed by the fried egg and a little black pepper. Spoon a small amount of tomato sauce on the inside of the muffin lid, then place on top of the egg and serve.

Full Australian Breakfast

An ever-so-slightly healthier way to start the day...

SERVES 4

120 g (4½ oz) ghee
200 g (7 oz) grey ghost mushrooms
    or best available
sea salt flakes and freshly cracked
    black pepper
50 g (1¾ oz) butter
160 g (5½ oz) Swordfish Bacon
    (see page 60)
4 Fish Sausages (see page 206)
4 eggs
4 × 1 cm (½ in) thick slices of rye
    baguette
100 ml (3½ fl oz) extra-virgin olive oil
4 curly parsley sprigs

Eel hash browns

6 waxy potatoes, such as desiree,
    peeled
½ smoked eel, skin and bones
    reserved and flesh shredded
    with a fork
50 g (1¾ oz/⅓ cup) plain
    (all-purpose) flour
1½ teaspoons salt
1½ teaspoons caster (superfine) sugar
1 tablespoon skim milk powder
2 eggs
1 litre (34 fl oz/4 cups) canola
    (rapeseed) oil, for deep-frying

Smoked heart baked beans

100 ml (3½ fl oz) extra-virgin olive oil
1 red onion, finely diced
1 garlic clove, grated preferably on
    a microplane
½ red long chilli, seeds removed
½ teaspoon smoked paprika
350 ml (12 fl oz) tomato passata
    (pureed tomatoes)
400 g (14 oz) cooked and drained
    cannellini beans
sea salt flakes and freshly cracked
    black pepper
1 smoked Spanish mackerel heart,
    grated preferably on a microplane

ALTERNATIVE FISH:
Smoked anchovies
Smoked sardines
Smoked sprats

For the hash browns, bring the potatoes and the skin and bones from the smoked eel, if available, to the boil in a large pot. Cover and cook for 5 minutes. Drain and cool, then grate the potatoes on a box grater into a bowl, add the remaining ingredients and shape the mixture into 110 g (4 oz) pucks.

Heat the oil for deep-frying in a large saucepan over a medium–high heat until it reaches a temperature of 180°C (350°F). Deep-fry the hash browns for 2–3 minutes until golden, then drain on paper towel. Season with sea salt.

For the baked beans, preheat the oven to 180°C (350°F).

Heat the olive oil in a large pot and cook the onion, garlic, chilli and smoked paprika for 5 minutes, stirring until the onion is beginning to soften. Add the passata with a splash of water and the drained beans. Season lightly with salt, the mackerel heart and pepper and stir well. Bring to the boil, then tip the mixture into a baking dish and cook in the oven for 1 hour to reduce and thicken. Keep warm.

Heat a small amount of ghee in a large frying pan over a high heat and wait until there is a light haze over the pan. Season the mushrooms lightly, then sauté for 1 minute. Add a small knob of butter and some black pepper. Tip into a bowl and keep warm.

Heat a little ghee in another frying pan over a medium heat and cook the bacon for 3 minutes until caramelised and crisp. Set aside and keep warm. Repeat with the fish sausages, cooking for 3–4 minutes until crisp and coloured. Set aside and keep warm. Crack the eggs into the pan and cook to your desired degree of doneness. Keep warm.

Heat a chargrill pan over a high heat, brush the rye bread with olive oil and grill until toasted. Arrange on warmed serving plates, top with a spoonful of the warm beans, mushrooms, a sausage, bacon, a fried egg and an eel hash brown, then garnish with parsley. Serve with a Bloody Mary.

See photo on following pages.

KGW Kiev

Growing up, chicken Kiev was always seen as a fancy dinner option and not eaten very often. Thinking about how we could apply this technique to a fish, we decided on quite possibly Australia's best table fish – the King George whiting. At the restaurant we have the ability to source transglutimate, which helps bind proteins together, so that we can remove all the bones and cartilage and create a seamless finish that holds the butter inside the fish. For a domestic-style recipe, the dish has been held together with toothpicks while frying. Taste and adjust the butter before filling and increase or decrease the garlic to suit your preferences.

SERVES 4

4 boneless butterflied King George
    whiting or other whiting, about
    250 g (9 oz)
150 g (5½ oz/1 cup) plain
    (all-purpose) flour
4 eggs, lightly whisked
180 g (6½ oz/3 cups) white panko
    breadcrumbs
2 litres (68 fl oz/8 cups) cottonseed
    or sunflower oil, for deep-frying
Lemon halves and green salad leaves,
    to serve

Garlic butter

60 g (2 oz) salted butter, softened
1 tablespoon flat-leaf (Italian) parsley,
    finely chopped
1 tablespoon chives, finely chopped
2 garlic cloves, grated preferably on
    a microplane

For the garlic butter, stir all the ingredients together until well mixed, then place on a piece of plastic wrap and roll into a long log, 1 cm (½ in) wide. Freeze until firm, then cut into four even barrels.

Lay the fish out in front of you with the heads away from you. Position the frozen garlic butter in the centre of the fish, then pull up the belly to completely enclose the butter. Position five toothpicks along the belly cavity to hold in place without any gaps. Excepting the head, coat the fish in the flour, then in the eggs and then in the breadcrumbs. Repeat with the remaining fish. Chill for 30 minutes.

Heat the oil for deep-frying in a large, heavy-based saucepan until the temperature reaches 180°C (350°F) on a cooking thermometer. Deep-fry two whiting for 4 minutes. Remove carefully and take out the toothpicks. Repeat with the other two fish.

Serve whole with a lemon half and your favourite green salad.

ALTERNATIVE FISH:
Herring
Mullet
Other whiting

Swordfish Saltimbocca

The pairing of sage and bacon still exists in this swordfish take on the classic recipe. Take care not to cook the fish too long here and serve with lemon wedges or a salad of herbs and dried tomatoes.

SERVES 2

12 large sage leaves
2 x 160 g (5½ oz) swordfish loin
    steaks, centre cut, about 2 cm
    (¾ in) thick
100 g (3½ oz) Swordfish Bacon
    (see page 60), cut into 10 strips,
    15 cm (6 in) long and 1 cm
    (½ in) wide
60 g (2 oz) ghee

Position six sage leaves on one of the swordfish steaks to cover the whole surface, then drape five slices of the bacon over the top creating even intervals between each piece of bacon. Fold the bacon around the swordfish and, using a toothpick, hold the bacon in place. Repeat with the second swordfish piece.

Heat the ghee in a frying pan over a medium heat and fry the saltimbocca, sage side down, for 3 minutes, or until golden brown. Turn on the other side and cook for 2–3 minutes more depending on the thickness of the fish. Remove from the pan, remove the toothpicks and leave to rest for a few minutes before serving.

ALTERNATIVE FISH:
Leatherjacket
Monkfish
Whiting

Smoked Eel & Beetroot Jam Doughnut

This savoury mouthful of smoke, salt, sweet, sour and creaminess is such a great way to start a meal, or even for a snack when only a doughnut will do.

MAKES APPROXIMATELY 30 DOUGHNUTS

Smoked eel filling

2 waxy potatoes, such as desiree, peeled and quartered
50 g (1¾ oz/¼ cup) fine salt
½ hot-smoked eel, skin and bones reserved and flesh mashed finely with a fork
250 g (9 oz/1 cup) sour cream
sea salt flakes and freshly cracked black pepper
lemon juice, to taste
pinch of freshly grated nutmeg

Beetroot puree

1 large red beetroot (beet), tops off
sea salt flakes
1½ tablespoons extra-virgin olive oil
2 lemon thyme sprigs
80 g (2¾ oz/⅓ cup) caster (superfine) sugar
50 ml (1¾ fl oz) red-wine vinegar

Doughnuts

30 g (1 oz) fresh yeast
135 ml (4½ fl oz) water
525 g (1 lb 3 oz/3½ cups) baker's or strong bread flour, plus extra for dusting
60 ml (2 fl oz/¼ cup) full-cream (whole) milk
85 g (3 oz/⅓ cup) caster (superfine) sugar
115 g (4 oz) egg yolks
60 g (2 oz) ghee, melted
2 teaspoons salt
2 litres (68 fl oz/8 cups) cottonseed or sunflower oil, for deep-frying

To make the filling, add the potatoes, salt and skin and bones from the smoked eel, if available, to a large saucepan filled with water and bring to the boil. Cook until the potato is completely soft, then drain, discarding the skin and bones. Push the potato through a sieve and cool until warm.

Add the mashed eel flesh and sour cream to the potato with a little salt, pepper and lemon juice to taste and combine well. Transfer the mixture to a piping (icing) bag fitted with a fine tip nozzle and chill.

For the beetroot puree, preheat the oven to 180°C (350°F).

Place the beetroot in the centre of a square of aluminium foil, season lightly with salt, olive oil and the thyme sprigs and bake for 40 minutes, or until completely soft. While hot, peel the skin off and cut into quarters, then blitz in a food processor or blender to a fine puree. Pass through a sieve and set aside.

Melt the sugar in a small pan for 8 minutes, or until it starts to become very dark. Add the vinegar and cook to melt the sugar again. Add the beetroot puree and cook over a medium heat for 10 minutes to thicken. Cool completely, then transfer to a piping bag fitted with a fine tip nozzle and set aside.

For the doughnuts, mix 15 g (½ oz) of the fresh yeast, the water and 150 g (5½ oz/1 cup) of the baker's flour together in a bowl until they are just combined. Leave for 2 hours at room temperature.

In a stand mixer bowl, combine the milk with the remaining yeast and leave for 1 minute. Add the remaining ingredients except the oil together with the first yeast mix and mix with the dough hook attachment for 5–7 minutes until the dough is shiny and well combined. Cover and leave to rise in the refrigerator overnight until it has doubled in size.

The next day, lightly flour a baking tray. Turn the dough out onto a lightly floured work surface and roll out to 1.5 cm (½ in) thickness. Using a 4 cm (1½ in) ring cutter, cut out circles and transfer them to the floured tray. Chill for 1 hour.

Heat the oil for deep-frying in a large, heavy-based saucepan until the temperature reaches 180°C (350°F). Using a slotted spoon, deep-fry a few doughnuts at a time on each side for 1–1½ minutes until golden brown and the centre is light and fluffy. Drain on paper towel.

Make a small hole in the top of each doughnut and fill with the filling to just below the top, then top it off by piping in a little beetroot puree. Serve warm.

ALTERNATIVE FISH:
Smoked anchovy
Smoked herring
Smoked sardine

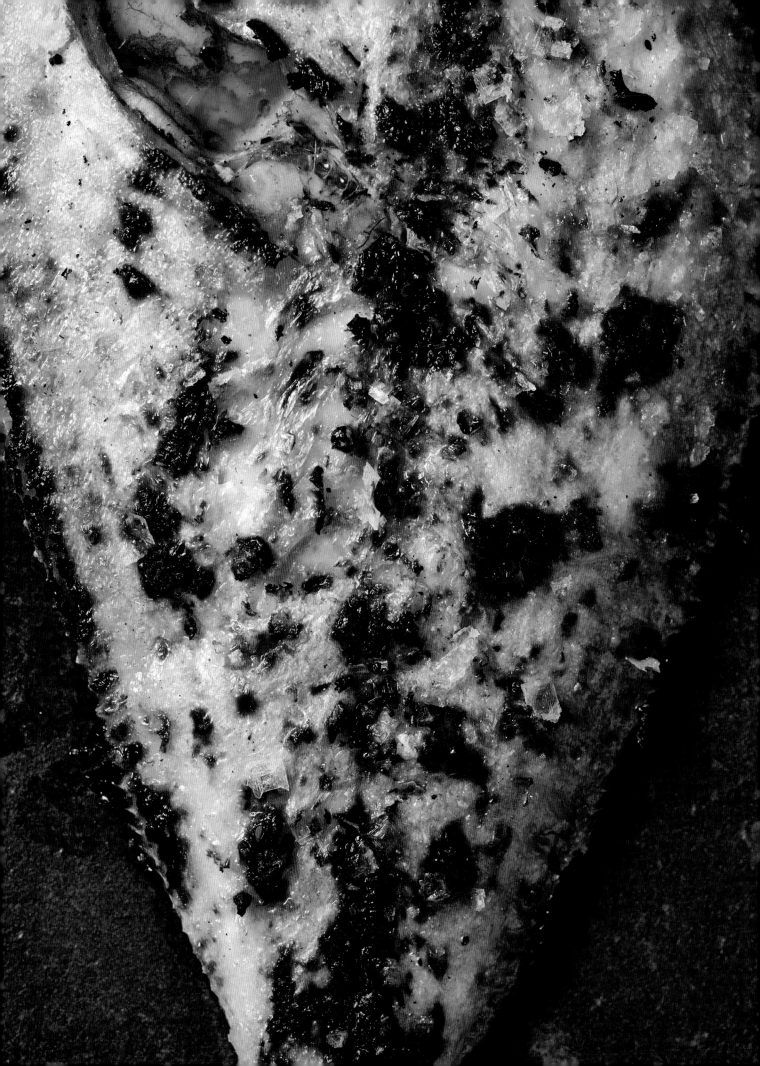

BBQ & GRILL

Great fish for barbecuing
and grilling include:

Bonito

Flounder

Herring

Mackerel

Mullet

Sardines

Spot whiting

Charcoal grilling or barbecuing can be either a fast, high heat method of cookery or a subtle way of gently finishing the crisp fish skin achieved in a pan to become even crisper. When fish comes into contact with the intense heat of a grill, the skin of the fish will immediately begin to blister, bubble and caramelise. Fish with a lot of natural fat and that aren't too thick are perfect for grilling.

Along with choosing a fish that has a good amount of natural fat, the key to grilling fish is patience. Try not to disturb the grilling process too often to check to see if your fish is stuck, as checking too early will result in the skin catching and ripping (while this is not the end of the world, aesthetically and also texturally it's far more pleasing for it to be intact). Becoming more confident grilling on your barbecue or charcoal grill will give you a huge advantage in terms of transforming the less desirable cheaper species of fish into something completely unrivalled – if correctly handled and cookery carefully considered, species such as herring, mullet, flounder, mackerel, sardines and spot whiting can all go toe to toe with the coral trouts, trumpeters and breams of this world.

Left, overleaf & page 182: Yellowbelly flounder.

BBQ BUTTERFLIED FISH ESSENTIALS

The key point to consider when grilling fish is to be sure you select a fish that has a good amount of natural fat – this will act as a lubricant to minimise the risk of the skin sticking on the grill racks as well as help to keep the flesh moist. Extra-virgin olive oil or grapeseed oil are good fats for grilling and should be lightly brushed over the skin of the fish along with a liberal pinch of sea salt flakes. Too much oil on the skin over the grill will cause flames to flare up and run the risk of the fish tasting of your chosen fuel.

If using charcoal beads or wood that has burnt down to charcoal when barbecuing, make sure the coals have burnt down to embers and there are no open flames coming from them. Spread the embers over the base of the grill evenly to avoid hot spots, which may make the skin burn or cook unevenly, and make sure the rack that you are grilling on is hot and has been sitting over the hot embers for at least 20 minutes before cooking.

1. Place the fish fillet, skin side down, on the grill rack and place a fish weight on top of the thickest side of the fish. (If using a softer-textured fish such as sardines or blue mackerel then use a small tray or pan on top.)

2. Remove the fish weight when the desired colour has been reached on the skin and check with the back of your hand to make sure the flesh is warm and has begun to change colour from raw to translucent. (If you find the flesh is too cold and not enough heat has travelled through it to warm the top of the fish, then work over less hot coals or fewer coals).

3. As soon as the fish is 75 per cent cooked, using a wide palette knife, take it carefully off the grill and place it on a warmed serving plate. Brush the skin with a little olive oil and season with sea salt. Allowing the fish to sit on a warm plate will give it the chance to set through to its optimum eating temperature. Don't go flipping the fish to the flesh side, as this will be detrimental to the fish's texture.

Left: Yellow-eye mullet (aged 4 days).

BBQ WHOLE FLAT FISH ESSENTIALS

The same technique applies for a flat fish on the grill as a fillet. The only difference is that when cooking a fish on the bone over the intense heat of a grill, a little more care needs to be taken.

Flounder, plaice, sole and turbot are all excellent fish for the grill as they require minimal labour before grilling and they have a great amount of gelatine within the skin along with a healthy fat content, which helps the fish to stay moist.

1.
A high heat is needed to colour the skin and minimise the risk of it sticking, but not too high that the skin burns and the fish remains raw on the bone. The position of coals is important. Have a few hot embers positioned in the centre of the grill and the rest built up around the edges. This way, the fish will colour and cook evenly.

2.
Once both sides of the fish have taken on good colour, check the internal temperature that sits on the bone near the head. It should reach 60°C (140°F).

3.
Brush with extra-virgin olive oil and season liberally with sea salt.

BBQ Red Mullet, Corn & Kelp Butter

The intoxicating aroma of red mullet cooking over a charcoal grill is enough to get anyone excited about this fish. I always refer to red mullet as poor man's lobster due to its distinct shellfish-like flavour, but this is a delicious dish that is rich, full of umami and sweetness from the corn as well as the skin of the fish.

SERVES 4

2 litres (68 fl oz/8 cups) water
100 g (3½ oz/⅓ cup) fine salt
4 ears of corn
90 ml (3 fl oz/⅓ cup) extra-virgin olive oil
sea salt flakes and freshly cracked black pepper
200 g (7 oz) butter, softened
2 tablespoons ground dried kelp (or use nori or wakame)
100 ml (3½ fl oz) Brown Fish Stock (see page 67)
lemon juice, to taste
4 boneless butterflied red mullet, about 200 g (7 oz) each, skin on, head and tail on

For the charcoal grill, make sure the grill is hot and the charcoal has cooked down to hot embers that have levelled out so the heat is even.

Bring the water and fine salt to the boil in a large saucepan over a high heat. Add the corn, cover and cook for 4 minutes, or until tender. Cool completely, then strip the husk from the corn, brush the kernels with 30 ml (1 fl oz) of the olive oil and season with sea salt.

Make sure the heat of the grill is even and you know where the hot spots of the grill are. Grill the corn on the grill rack for 4 minutes, or until lightly blackened and charred all over. Remove from the grill and strip the kernels from the cob. Set aside.

Whisk the butter in a stand mixer fitted with the whisk attachment until pale and doubled in volume. Add the ground kelp and mix until it is incorporated.

Heat the stock and corn kernels in a saucepan until the stock is reduced by half. Dice the kelp butter and add it piece by piece to the stock, swirling the pot over a low heat until the butter is emulsified. The sauce should be thick and shiny. Season with lemon juice, pepper and a little salt. Keep warm.

Brush the fish with the remaining olive oil and season the skin liberally with salt. Place the fish, skin side down, on the grill rack, add a fish weight on top of the flesh closest to the head and grill for 2 minutes. Reposition the weight to the centre of the fish and cook for a further minute.

When the fish is 70 per cent cooked, remove it from the grill. Divide the corn and kelp butter sauce between plates and lay over the fish to serve.

ALTERNATIVE FISH:
Herring
Mullet
Whiting

BBQ Glazed Bar Cod Ribs

This dish is best prepared when working with a larger fish species, such as bar cod, bass grouper, hapuka or mulloway, as they have a significant rib cage as opposed to smaller fish. These are best enjoyed hot from the grill simply with a good squeeze of lime, cutlery optional.

SERVES 4

4 bar cod ribs, about 100 g (3½ oz)
   each
2 tablespoons extra-virgin olive oil
sea salt flakes

BBQ sauce

500 g (1 lb 2 oz) tomatoes, blistered
   over charcoal
100 ml (3½ fl oz) malt vinegar
150 g (5½ oz/¾ cup) dark muscovado
   (soft brown) sugar
½ teaspoon ground star anise
½ teaspoon ground fennel seeds
½ teaspoon ground coriander seeds,
½ teaspoon ground black
   peppercorns
½ teaspoon ground smoked paprika
2½ tablespoons worcestershire sauce
1 tablespoon Vegemite

For the sauce, blitz all the ingredients together in a blender or food processor to a puree, then pour into a large saucepan and cook over a medium heat for 40 minutes until thick and fragrant. Return to the blender and blend until completely smooth. Leave to cool.

Once cool, cover the bar cod ribs with the sauce and chill overnight.

The next day, for the charcoal grill, make sure the grill is hot and the charcoal has cooked down to hot embers that have levelled out so the heat is even.

Remove the ribs from the marinade, scraping away the excess, then brush them with a little olive oil and season with sea salt.

Making sure the heat of the grill is even and you know where the hot spots are, arrange the ribs on the grill rack and cook over a high heat until they are well caramelised top and bottom.

Serve immediately, making sure finger bowls and warm hand towels are within easy reach.

ALTERNATIVE FISH:
Grouper
Hake
Hapuka

Tommy Ruff, Macadamia Tahini & Lemon Yoghurt

The richness of Australia's favourite nut, the macadamia, and the acidity and floral aroma of lemon yoghurt compliment this beautiful underused species of fish. Tommy ruff (or Australian herring) has a very clean, briny flavour and is full of good oils. It is a perfect fish for the grill.

SERVES 4

4 small broccolini stems
2 tablespoons extra-virgin olive oil
sea salt flakes
4 butterflied Tommy ruff (herring)
lemon juice, to taste

Lemon yoghurt

1 lemon, preferably Meyer
250 g (9 oz/1 cup) natural yoghurt,
    plus extra if necessary
sea salt flakes

Macadamia tahini

250 g (9 oz/1½ cups) macadamia nuts

Prepare a small charcoal grill, gas barbecue or chargrill pan for grilling the fish. (I suggest a small charcoal grill for best results.)

To make the lemon yoghurt, using a small knife, prick small holes over the lemon, then add to a saucepan and cover with cold water. Cover, bring to the boil and cook for 5 minutes. Drain the lemon and repeat this process two more times. This will result in the lemon being very soft and nearly all the bitterness of the pith will have been removed. Cut the lemon in half and remove the seeds, then blitz in a blender until very smooth. Transfer to a bowl, cover with baking paper to prevent a skin forming and chill.

Once the puree is completely chilled, mix with the yoghurt and a generous pinch of salt. If the flavour is still too strong add a little more yoghurt. Set aside.

For the tahini, preheat the oven to 160°C (325°F). Roast the macadamias on a baking tray for 15 minutes, or until a light tan colour. Tip the hot nuts into a Thermomix set to 70°C (158°F) and blend for 10 minutes until completely smooth and the consistency of peanut butter. Alternatively, blitz in a blender with a little warm water.

For the charcoal grill, make sure the grill is hot and the charcoal has cooked down to hot embers.

Brush the broccolini stems with a little olive oil and season with sea salt. Grill over a medium–high heat for 2 minutes, or until tender. Finely cut the stems into small discs while stopping short of the florets and set these aside in a warmed bowl.

Brush the herring skin with a little oil and salt, then grill, skin side down, on the grill racks over a very high heat for 2 minutes being careful not to burn the skin. When the fish is 70 per cent cooked remove from the rack and fold over so the fillets are sandwiched together.

To serve, place a spoonful of the tahini in the centre of a plate and spoon a small spoonful of the lemon yoghurt inside. Brush the broccolini with a little more oil and season with lemon juice. Place a pile of the cut stems and small florets on top of the sauces, then add the herring alongside.

ALTERNATIVE FISH:
Mackerel
Kingfish
Sardines

Greenback Flounder in Verjuice & Sorrel

I have the privilege of working with the fisherman Bruce Collis of Corner Inlet in Victoria. His fish are truly unrivalled and the greenback flounder are remarkable. This is a fantastic preparation to show off the fish's elegant flavour and firm texture. Yellowbelly flounder, sole or turbot are all excellent substitutes.

SERVES 4

2 x 500 g (1 lb 2 oz oz) greenback
   flounder, gutted and scaled
120 ml (4 fl oz) extra-virgin olive oil
sea salt flakes
120 ml (4 fl oz) verjuice
130 g (4½ oz/1 cup) large leaf
   sorrel, sliced

For the charcoal grill, make sure the grill is hot and the charcoal has cooked down to hot embers.

Brush the flounder with a little olive oil all over the skin and season well with sea salt. Grill the flounders directly on the grill rack on the white side (or bottom side) for 4 minutes, then turn over and cook for a further 4 minutes, or until the internal temperature on the bone reaches 60°C (140°F) on a probe thermometer.

Put the remaining olive oil and the verjuice on a flat baking tray and warm the tray on the side of the hot grill. Transfer the flounder to the warm tray and leave to rest off the heat for 5 minutes.

Position the flounder, white side up, on a flat plate. Return the baking tray to the hot grill and, using a whisk, mix the fish juices into the verjuice and olive oil, then spoon over the flounder. Finish with a big handful of sorrel leaves.

ALTERNATIVE FISH:
Yellowbelly flounder
Sole
Turbot

BBQ Swordfish Chop with Tomato & Peach Salad

Swordfish is the fish that really gave me the inspiration to merge the meat world with fish. It is also a great example of how we approach cooking at Saint Peter. When butchering swordfish we leave a quarter of the top loin on the bone and remove the other three loins. By leaving a quarter on the bone, you then have a unique cut of fish, which essentially becomes a standing rib of swordfish. We cure the bellies and smoke them to then be diced and stirred through a bordelaise sauce made from the roasted swordfish bones and the bone marrow from within the spine. The rib, meanwhile, sometimes gets cut up into chops like this one, served with my favourite salad.

SERVES 4

1 x 1.5 kg (3 lb 5 oz) swordfish steak
　　on the bone (ideally aged 20 days)
2 tablespoons extra-virgin olive oil
sea salt flakes and freshly cracked
　　black pepper

Ox heart tomato & white peach salad

175 ml (6 fl oz) extra-virgin olive oil
50 ml (1¾ fl oz) chardonnay vinegar
　　or white-wine vinegar with a pinch
　　of sugar
½ vanilla bean, seeds scraped
3 large ox heart tomatoes
　　(beef tomatoes), sliced
sea salt flakes and freshly cracked
　　black pepper
3 white peaches, sliced the same size
　　as the tomatoes

For the charcoal grill, make sure the grill is hot and the charcoal has cooked down to hot embers.

To make the salad, combine the olive oil, vinegar and vanilla together in a bowl. Season the tomatoes well with salt and pepper and arrange on a serving plate with the peaches. Whisk the dressing to combine, then spoon over the tomatoes and peaches. Set aside.

Preheat the oven to 100°C (212°F) or lower if possible.

To grill the steak, start by placing the chop on a wire rack set inside a tray. Brush the flesh with a little olive oil and season liberally with sea salt. Gently warm in the oven until the internal temperature is 35°C (95°F) when measured with a probe thermometer. The fish should still look very rare.

Transfer the steak to the grill rack and cook over a very high heat for 2 minutes on each side, including the skin and bone side, being careful not to burn the skin. Check the internal temperature, it needs to be at a temperature of 55°C (131°F). Leave to rest for 5 minutes.

Once rested, brush the steak with a little more olive oil, season with sea salt and pepper, then carve the eye of the muscle from the bone leaving the L-shaped bone left behind. Season this bone liberally with salt and pepper and position it on the centre of a plate.

Carve the steak into thin slices then re-assemble the fish back to the bone on the plate and serve with the tomato and peach salad.

ALTERNATIVE FISH:
Moonfish
Tuna
Wild Kingfish

BBQ Blue Mackerel & Burnt Tomato on Toast

A burnt tomato has never tasted so good. This dressing is a delicious accompaniment for richer flavoured fish like mackerel, tuna or herring, but make sure to only half-cook the mackerel on the grill and allow the warmth of the tomatoes and the hot toast to finish the cooking.

SERVES 4

1 x 300 g (10½ oz) blue mackerel
60 ml (2 fl oz/¼ cup) extra-virgin olive oil
sea salt flakes and freshly cracked black pepper
2 slices good-quality sourdough bread

Tomato dressing

300 g (10½ oz) cherry tomatoes, halved
75 g (2¾ oz/½ cup) capers
125 g (4½ oz) French shallots, finely sliced into rings
2 teaspoons caster (superfine) sugar
100 ml (3½ fl oz) chardonnay vinegar or white-wine vinegar with a pinch of sugar
50 ml (1¾ fl oz) Fish Garum (see page 73)
200 ml (7 fl oz) extra-virgin olive oil

For the dressing, burn the tomato halves, cut side down, in batches if necessary, in a heavy, cast-iron pan over a high heat for 6 minutes, or until softened. Once all the tomatoes are burnt, add the remaining ingredients and leave for 30 minutes before serving. Keep warm.

Place the mackerel in the middle of a chopping board with the tail facing you and the belly cavity exposed and open. Using a sharp knife, cut down one side of the central spine and remove the fillet as you would if you were going through the top side of the fish, but when you reach the point where the fillet is off but still attached to the head, turn the fish so the head is now facing you and, using the top third of the knife, split the head in half. This will result in a fillet that still has the tail and the head intact. Remove the pin bones. Repeat on the other side, but this time lay the fish flat to the work surface and cut the fillet through the top of the fish ensuring that the head and tail are still attached to the fillet. (If this is too challenging, just remove the fillets as you would normally or get your fish shop to do this.)

For the charcoal grill, make sure the grill is hot and the charcoal has cooked down to hot embers.

Brush the skin of the mackerel with a little olive oil and season with sea salt. Grill on the skin for 2–3 minutes until coloured and the flesh is warm to the touch, then remove and brush the fish skin with a little more olive oil and season with a little more salt and a touch of pepper.

Brush the bread with olive oil and grill for 1 minute on each side until smoky and well coloured. Arrange the toast on a plate, spoon the tomato dressing over the toast, then place the mackerel on top. Serve whole or cut to share with friends.

ALTERNATIVE FISH:
Mullet
Herring
Sardines

BBQ Sand Whiting, Peas, Swordfish Bacon & Lettuce

Sand whiting has a beautiful sweet flesh that works so well with sweet juicy spring peas and the crunch of lettuce leaves. The addition of the swordfish bacon brings so much savouriness and seasoning to the dish, which is brightened by the use of verjuice and tarragon. This is a perfect spring dish.

SERVES 4

2 litres (68 fl oz/8 cups) water
100 g (3½ oz/⅓ cup) fine salt
400 g (14 oz/2½ cups) fresh peas
60 g (2 oz) ghee
200 g (7 oz) Swordfish Bacon
    (see page 60), cut into 2 cm
    (¾ in) matchsticks
120 ml (4 fl oz) verjuice
300 ml (10 fl oz) Brown Fish Stock
    (see page 67)
4 heads baby gem lettuce, halved
    and washed
1 tablespoon picked tarragon leaves
80 g (2¾ oz) butter
sea salt flakes and freshly cracked
    black pepper
4 × 200 g (7 oz) reverse butterflied
    sand whiting or whiting
3 tablespoons extra-virgin olive oil

For the charcoal grill, make sure the grill is hot and the charcoal has cooked down to hot embers.

For the peas, have a bowl of iced water to hand. Bring the water and fine salt to the boil in a large stockpot over a high heat. Add the peas, cover and cook for 3 minutes, or until tender. Drain and refresh in the bowl of iced water.

Heat the ghee in a frying pan and fry the bacon for 5 minutes, or until a deep golden brown. Pour in the verjuice and stir, scraping up the bits that have stuck to the bottom of the pan. Cook for 3 minutes until it is reduced to a syrup.

Add the stock, then add the lettuce and cover with baking paper. Cook gently for 2 minutes until the lettuce has only just collapsed. Add the peas, tarragon and butter, then season to taste. Keep warm.

Brush the butterflied fish with olive oil and season with salt. Position the fish evenly across the grill rack and grill with fish weights on top of the flesh for 2 minutes, or until the skin is bubbled and charred and the flesh is warm. Remove from the heat.

Spoon the peas, bacon and lettuce over four warmed serving bowls or plates and place the half-cooked fish on top to finish cooking.

ALTERNATIVE FISH:
Flounder
Mackerel

BBQ Mahi-Mahi Rack, Spiced Broad Bean Leaves, Carrots & Mead

I've used mahi-mahi in this recipe as it reminds me so much of a lamb rack, with the robust spices and the sweetness of carrot and mead taking it to a very different savoury dimension. There is such a big difference in the fish's flavour and texture profile as well when it's cooked on the bone like this.

SERVES 2

2 x 300 g (10 oz) mahi-mahi racks
1 tablespoon extra-virgin olive oil
sea salt flakes
100 ml (3½ fl oz) Brown Fish Stock
    (ideally mahi-mahi, see page 67)

Carrot butter

1 kg (2 lb 3 oz) carrots, coarsely
    chopped
150 ml (5 fl oz) mead, plus extra
    to season
200 g (7 oz) butter, softened

Spiced broad bean leaves

300 g (10 oz) broad (fava) bean leaves
1 tablespoon dried crushed chilli
1 tablespoon sweet paprika
1 teaspoon finely diced fresh ginger
½ teaspoon saffron threads
4 French shallots, finely diced
2 fresh bay leaves, finely sliced into
    long strips
1 tablespoon ground cumin
2 garlic cloves, finely grated
2 tablespoons finely chopped flat-leaf
    (Italian) parsley
2 tablespoons finely chopped
    coriander (cilantro)
½ preserved lemon, finely sliced
125 ml (4½ fl oz/½ cup) olive oil,
    plus extra for brushing
juice of ½ lemon

To make the carrot butter, have a bowl of iced water to hand. Blitz the carrots and mead in a food processor to a fine pulp. Push this pulp through a fine-mesh sieve into a large saucepan, then cook over a medium heat until the carrot juice is reduced to a syrup, about 100 ml (3½ fl oz). Transfer the syrup to a bowl and chill over the bowl of iced water.

Whisk the softened butter in a stand mixer for 10 minutes, or until very pale and nearly doubled in volume. Add the carrot syrup and mix for a further 1 minute. Transfer to a bowl and chill until required.

For the spiced broad bean leaves, combine all the ingredients except the broad bean leaves in a bowl to make a dressing. Leave to stand at room temperature until required.

For the charcoal grill, make sure the grill is hot and the charcoal has cooked down to hot embers.

Brush the fish skin with the olive oil and season with sea salt. Divide the coals to create a slightly cooler area and a more intense side of the grill. Start grilling the skin over a high heat for 4 minutes to develop a good colour, then turn to the bone side of the rack, transfer to the slightly cooler side of the grill and cook for a further 6 minutes. The ideal internal temperature should come to 50°C (122°F) when measured with a probe thermometer. Remove and leave to rest.

In a pan, cook the fish stock for 5 minutes, or until it has reduced down to a syrupy glaze. Add small cubes of the carrot butter while swirling the pan to emulsify the butter into the stock. Season with mead and a splash of lemon juice. Keep warm.

Brush the broad bean leaves with a little extra olive oil and place inside a sieve. Holding the handle of the sieve, gently grill the leaves for 1 minute until tender, then transfer to a bowl and dress with a few tablespoons of the dressing (the rest of the dressing will keep refrigerated for a few days and is great for breakfast spooned over a poached egg). Serve the fish with the vegetables and the warm carrot and mead sauce.

ALTERNATIVE FISH:
Flounder
Swordfish
Wild Kingfish

Yellowfin Tuna Cheeseburger with Salt & Vinegar Onion Rings

A fish burger that looks and tastes like a beef burger. The first time we cooked and ate this, I couldn't believe what I was eating. I would happily choose this over a typical burger any day of the week.

SERVES 4

4 slices cheddar cheese
4 white burger buns, halved
60 ml (2 fl oz/¼ cup) BBQ sauce
    (see page 187)
12 discs of Lacto-fermented
    cucumbers (see page 101)
4 slices Swordfish Bacon
    (see page 60), fried until crisp
    (optional)
4 trimmed iceberg lettuce leaves
sea salt flakes

Patties

40 g (1½ oz) ghee
200 g (7 oz) French shallots,
    finely diced
100 g (3½ oz) yellowfin tuna
    trimmings
1 tablespoon salt
200 g (7 oz) yellowfin tuna loin
200 g (7 oz) yellowfin tuna red muscle
1 teaspoon ground black pepper
½ teaspoon ground fennel seeds
50 g (1¾ oz) diced Murray cod, cobia
    or hake fat
2 tablespoons extra-virgin olive oil

Salt & vinegar onion rings

2 tablespoons caster (superfine) sugar
500 ml (17 fl oz/2 cups) malt vinegar
80 g (2¾ oz/¼ cup) salt
4 onions, sliced into 1 cm (½ in) thick
    slices, tiny centre rings removed
2 litres (68 fl oz/8 cups) cottonseed
    or sunflower oil, for deep-frying
50 g (1¾ oz/¼ cup) rice flour
½ quantity Fish & Chips batter
    (see page 139)

For the patties, heat the ghee in a saucepan over a low heat, add the shallot, cover with a lid and leave to sweat for 10 minutes without colouring. Blend the tuna trimmings with the salt in a food processor to form a pink paste.

Coarsely chop the tuna loin into a mix that resembles beef mince. Do the same to the red muscle, then stir this into the paste with the tuna loin. Add the pepper and fennel, then the diced Murray cod fat. Chill for at least 30 minutes.

For the charcoal grill, make sure the grill is hot and the charcoal has cooked down to hot embers.

Shape the tuna mix into four patties, weighing 120 g (4 oz) each, pressing them down lightly so the thickness doesn't exceed 2 cm (¾ in). Brush with the oil and leave at room temperature before grilling.

Grill the patties on the grill rack for 4 minutes until well caramelised on both sides. With a minute remaining on the second side, place the cheese slices on top and gently melt, then remove and leave to rest.

For the onion rings, bring the sugar, vinegar and salt to the boil in a pan. Separate the onion into individual rings, then cook a handful of onion rings in the pickle liquid for 1–2 minutes until just softened. Remove with a slotted spoon and repeat until they are all cooked.

Heat the oil for deep-frying in a large, heavy-based saucepan until it reaches a temperature of 180°C (350°F) on a cooking thermometer. Dust the onion rings lightly in flour and coat in the batter. Drop each ring into the oil slowly and fry until light golden brown. Drain on paper towel and season with salt.

Lightly toast the burger buns over the grill. To assemble, put a spoonful of the BBQ sauce in the centre of a base, add a patty, followed by pickles, bacon, if using, lettuce, a little more sauce and the top of the bun. Press down and serve with the onion rings.

See photo on previous pages.

Moonfish Steak Frites

This fish version of steak frites carries the same weight of flavours and textures as the original. Even the most insatiable palates will be satisfied after eating this rich cut of fish. When considering accompaniments, the possibilities are endless.

SERVES 10

1 x 2 kg (4 lb 6 oz) moonfish (opah) or tuna (ideally aged 8 days) round muscle, dark meat, skin on
60 ml (2 fl oz/¼ cup) extra-virgin olive oil
sea salt flakes and freshly cracked black pepper

Bearnaise sauce

6 French shallots, sliced
4 tarragon sprigs, plus 2 tablespoons chopped tarragon
12 whole black peppercorns
250 ml (8½ fl oz/1 cup) white wine
250 ml (8½ fl oz/1 cup) tarragon vinegar
7 egg yolks
500 g (1 lb 2 oz) unsalted butter, cut into cubes, at room temperature
sea salt flakes and freshly cracked black pepper

To serve

120 g (4 oz/4 cups) picked watercress
80 g (2¾ oz/2 cups) picked frisée
10 radishes, cut into thin wedges
½ quantity Verjuice dressing (see page 90)
1 kg (2 lb 3 oz) potato chips (see page 139)

For the bearnaise, cook the shallots, tarragon sprigs, peppercorns, wine and vinegar in a saucepan over a medium–high heat for 8–10 minutes until the liquid is reduced to 150 ml (5 fl oz).

Place the egg yolks in a large heatproof bowl that sits easily over a saucepan. Strain the tarragon reduction, pour it over the egg yolks and whisk well. Place the bowl over a saucepan of barely simmering water and start whisking. When the mixture thickens by tripling in size, add the butter, 3–4 cubes at a time, still whisking well. When all the butter is added, remove the bowl from the heat, add the chopped tarragon and check the seasoning. Place baking paper on top to prevent a skin forming. Keep warm.

Preheat the oven to its lowest possible temperature. Brush the moonfish with olive oil and season with salt. Cook the fish on a wire rack set inside a baking tray in the oven for 1 hour until the internal temperature of the fish reaches 45°C (113°F) when tested with a probe thermometer. Leave to rest for at least 10 minutes, then brush the skin again with olive oil.

Heat a large cast-iron pan on the stove. Brown the fish skin until it is caramelised. Kiss the backside of the muscle in the pan but only briefly, then remove and cut long steaks from the fish, similar to cutting a beef rump cap (sirloin cap). Season and serve with the bearnaise sauce, a watercress, frisée and radish salad dressed with verjuice dressing and a pile of hot chips.

ALTERNATIVE FISH:
Marlin
Tuna
Swordfish

See photo on page 205.

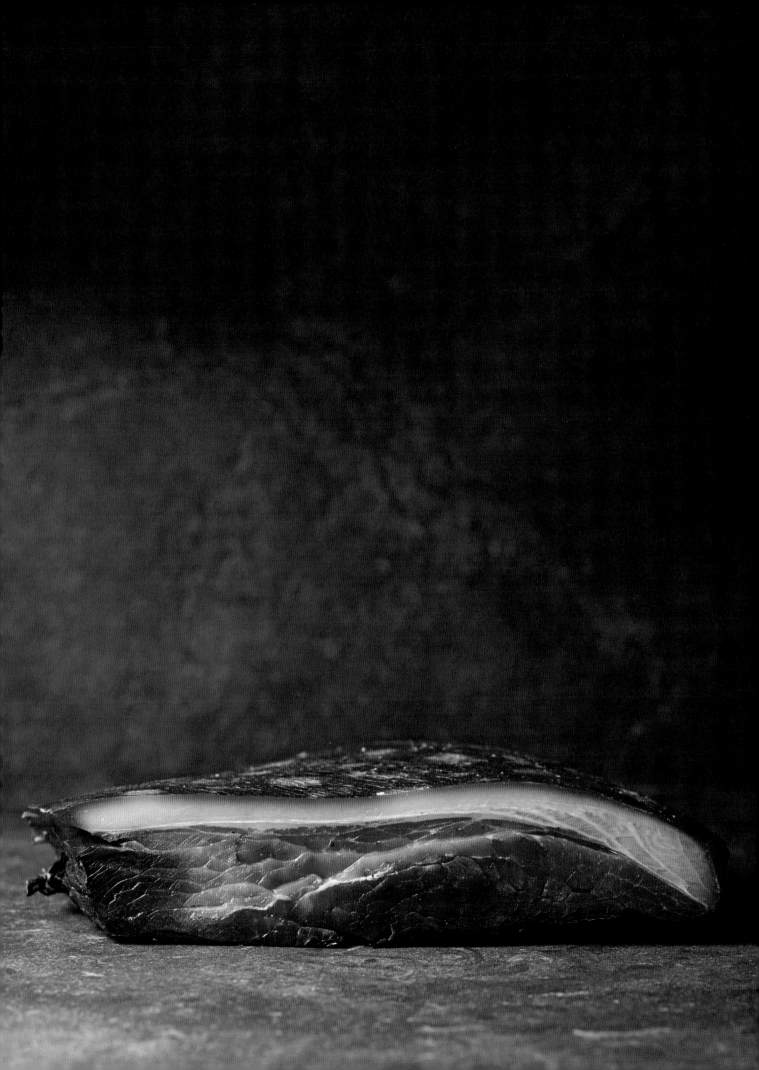

Grilled Sausage, Celeriac, Peas & Onion Sauce

There's nothing fancy about this combination of flavours – essentially, it's a recreation of the sausages, mash and onion gravy combo we all know and love with fish sausages substituting for the typical pork. I absolutely love this dish and I hope you do too.

SERVES 4

Sausages

40 g (1½ oz) ghee
3 onions, finely diced
250 g (9 oz) ocean trout or sea
    trout belly
250 g (9 oz) boneless, skinless white
    fish (such as ling, hake, cod, grouper
    or snapper), cut into 5 mm (¼ in) dice
1½ teaspoons fine salt
1 teaspoon ground black pepper
1 teaspoon ground fennel seeds
2 tablespoons finely chopped parsley
2 tablespoons finely chopped chives
natural lamb casings, soaked for
    about 45 minutes

Celeriac puree

375 g (13 oz) celeriac, peeled and
    cut into 2 cm (¾ in) cubes
200 ml (7 fl oz) milk
100 ml (3½ fl oz) thickened
    (double/heavy) cream
40 g (1½ oz) butter
sea salt flakes

Onion sauce

50 g (1¾ oz) butter
4 large onions, finely sliced
2 garlic cloves, sliced
1 fresh bay leaf
50 ml (1¾ fl oz) sherry vinegar
750 ml (25½ fl oz/3 cups) Brown Fish
    Stock (see page 67)
sea salt flakes and freshly cracked
    black pepper

Seasoned peas

200 g (7 oz/1¼ cups) peas, shelled
sea salt flakes and freshly cracked
    black pepper
60 ml (2 fl oz/¼ cup) extra-virgin olive oil

Heat the ghee in a small saucepan over a medium heat and sweat the onion for 6–7 minutes, then cool completely.

Dice the trout belly into large chunks and chill for at least 2 hours until completely cold.

Blend the trout belly in small batches in a food processor until smooth. If the mix seems too oily, add a splash of chilled water to help emulsify. Transfer to a bowl and add the diced white fish and all the seasonings including the onions and herbs.

Using a sausage filler fitted with an attachment wide enough to fit the diced fish through, add the sausage mix to the barrel. Force the mix through the filler and into the presoaked sausage casings and create 12–15 cm (4¾–6 in) lengths, tying them off as you go along. Once a batch is made, hang them on hooks or spread them out on a wire rack to dry, preferably overnight.

The next day, for the celeriac puree, combine the celeriac, milk, cream, butter and a little salt in a large, heavy-based saucepan. Bring to a gentle simmer over a medium heat, then reduce the heat and simmer gently, uncovered, stirring occasionally, for 20–25 minutes until the celeriac is very soft. Drain most of the liquid and set aside. Transfer the celeriac to a blender or food processor and blend until smooth. You may need some of the reserved cooking liquid. Season well and set aside warm.

For the onion sauce, melt the butter in a heavy-based saucepan over a low heat and cook the onions, garlic and bay leaf gently, covered with a lid, for 25 minutes, or until the onions are very soft. Uncover and cook for a further 15 minutes until the onions become caramelised. Pour in the vinegar, stirring to scrape up any bits that have stuck to the bottom of the pan and cook for 3 minutes, or until it has reduced to a syrup. Add the stock and cook over a medium heat for 20 minutes until reduced by half. Season well and keep warm.

For the charcoal grill, make sure the grill is hot and the charcoal has cooked down to hot embers that have levelled out so the heat is even.

Grill the sausages on the grill rack for 5–6 minutes, making sure the heat is kept moderate until the skins have set and the sausages are firm without much colour. Bring the coals together to create an intense heat and grill for 1 minute until all sides are coloured. Remove from the grill and leave to rest.

For the peas, blanch the peas in a large saucepan of boiling water with a generous pinch of salt for 2–3 minutes until tender and vibrant green. Remove and dress with a little olive oil, salt and pepper.

To serve, add a spoonful of the celeriac puree to the centre of a bowl followed by two sausages, the peas, onion sauce and a little extra-virgin olive oil.

BAKED & ROASTED

Great fish for baking/
roasting include:

Cod

Coral trout

Flathead

John dory

Murray cod

Ocean trout

Rainbow trout

Turbot

Swordfish

Unlike meat cookery where joints of meat are roasted over fire or in high-temperature ovens to break down connective tissue, fish needs to be handled with care. There is a huge importance on fish selection when applying this dry method of cookery. The fish suitable for roasting or baking is one that has good natural fat, such as cobia, trout, cod or a flat fish like turbot.

Salt crusts and en papilotte all help in making finer-textured and leaner species of fish, such as snapper, pearl perch and sea bream, highly delicious and very simple to prepare.

If roasting a fish whole on the bone, the fish itself has a vacant belly cavity, which is a great opportunity to add a huge amount of flavour.

Fragrant herbs, such as basil, bay, rosemary and thyme, are all perfect for more robust, fat-enriched fish species.

Roasting and baking fish shouldn't be limited just to a whole fish; flathead chops, john dory darnes and tuna heads are all magnificent roasted in both conventional and wood-burning ovens because of their fatty, gelatinous qualities. For best results, when cooking in this style, make sure you have a probe thermometer, as well as sea salt flakes, as it is important to season the fish well before roasting. A wire rack is also imperative to elevate the fish off the direct heat that a tray or pan would generate. This allows the heat to pass uniformly around the fish and cook it evenly.

Left, overleaf & page 212: Rock flathead (aged 5 days).

ROASTED ROUND FISH ESSENTIALS

There are two critical points to roasting a fish successfully. The first is the most important and that's choosing the right fish to suit this method of cookery. Second, heat control is key to keeping the flesh moist and the skin bronzed and crisp.

1. Preheat an oven to 100°C (212°F). Place a wire rack inside a baking tray. Lay the whole fish you are cooking, about 400 g (14 oz), flat on a work surface and fill the cavity with a selection of herbs and spices depending on the style of dish and what the species of fish is. Season the cavity of the fish as well as the skin with sea salt flakes. Dust the outside of the fish very lightly with 1 teaspoon milk powder. This will give you the option later to caramelise the skin.

2. Stand the fish up using the collars of the fish as a support and cook in the oven for 35–40 minutes until the fish reaches 55°C (131°F) on a probe thermometer. Remove the fish and leave to rest for 8–10 minutes.

3. The fish is ready to serve, but if you would like to have a golden brown skin then either preheat the oven to its highest setting with the grill or salamander switched on and grill on the wire rack for 2–3 minutes. Alternatively, heat 500 ml (17 fl oz/2 cups) canola (rapeseed) oil in saucepan to a temperature of 220°C (430°F) on the stove. Working with the fish still elevated off the baking tray, very carefully pour the hot oil over the cooked fish. It will blister the skin and cause the sugars in the milk powder to caramelise. Season the skin with sea salt flakes before serving.

John Dory Cooked in Kelp & Salt

I find this unfussed style of preparation so enjoyable at home as you have the ability to buy a whole fish, bones in, which is appropriate for the number of people you are cooking for. So whether it's a plate-sized john dory to be shared between two people or a whole Murray cod for six, this method will allow you to cover the whole fish top to bottom with salt, then bake it in the oven until done.

SERVES 5–6

pinch of sea salt flakes
cracked black pepper
3 kg (6 lb 10 oz) whole john dory, gutted
1 kg (2 lb 3 oz) table salt
200 ml (7 fl oz) water
1 bunch kelp or corn husks

Preheat the oven to 220°C (430°F).

Sprinkle the sea salt and some black pepper in the cavity of the fish. Spread a 2 cm (¾ in) layer of table salt over a large baking tray. Arrange the fish on top and sprinkle with a little water. Position the kelp leaves on top of the fish, covering as much of the skin top and bottom as possible, then cover the top with the rest of the table salt. Sprinkle some more water over the salt; this will help to form the crust.

Bake for 15 minutes, or until an internal temperature of 50°C (122°F) is reached on a probe thermometer. Remove and leave to rest for 15 minutes.

Break the crust from the top of the fish (the skin will probably come off with it). To fillet the fish, draw a line down the spine and remove the flesh in large chunks. Break the spine at the head and tail and remove. Take the fillets from the second side.

Divide the fish between serving plates, about 160 g (5½ oz) per serving.

ALTERNATIVE FISH:
Coral trout
Snapper
Turbot

See photo on previous page.

Roast Fish Bone Marrow, Harissa & Chickpea Pancake

Fish frames are always available at most good fish shops or markets. Make sure to request one that has not been soaked in water and has been freshly cut. The blood, which may be on the bone, must be vibrant and red, the bone should have clean, glassy meat still attached to it from the fillet and there should be no aroma. The flavour is meaty, yet quite mild but relies on the seasonings used. It is the texture that makes this particular cut of the fish so extraordinary.

SERVES 4

1 swordfish spine
sea salt flakes

Harissa

250 ml (8½ fl oz/1 cup) extra-virgin
    olive oil
2 garlic cloves, peeled
4 banana shallots, finely diced
1 long red chilli, seeds removed
    and charred
4 red capsicums (bell peppers), seeds
    removed, charred and peeled
2 teaspoons toasted cumin seeds
½ teaspoon toasted coriander seeds
1 tablespoon ground dried bush
    tomato (optional)
1 tablespoon tomato paste
    (concentrated puree)
2 tablespoons raw (demerara) sugar
100 ml (3½ fl oz) Fish Garum
    (see page 73)
sea salt flakes

Chickpea pancakes

200 g (7 oz/1¾ cups) chickpea
    (besan) flour
1 teaspoon salt, plus extra for
    seasoning
½ teaspoon cracked black pepper,
    plus extra for seasoning
450 ml (15 fl oz) water
1 tablespoon ghee, for cooking

Spice mix

1 teaspoon ground cumin
1 teaspoon ground toasted coriander
    seeds
½ teaspoon ground black pepper
1 teaspoon ground bush tomato,
    sumac or smoked paprika
1 teaspoon sea salt flakes

ALTERNATIVE FISH:
Bugfish
Mahi-mahi
Tuna

For the harissa, heat the olive oil in a pot over a medium–high heat and stir-fry the garlic and shallot for 1 minute. Add the grilled chilli, capsicum, toasted spices and bush tomato, if using, and cook for 5 minutes until fragrant. Add the tomato paste and cook over a medium heat for 3–4 minutes. Add the sugar and cook for 5 minutes, then add the garum and cook for a further 5 minutes. Season with salt and blitz in a blender until smooth, adding a little warm water, if necessary. Return the puree to a large saucepan and fry for 5–10 minutes until the colour deepens and the paste is fragrant. Store in a sealed sterilised jar in the refrigerator until needed.

For the pancakes, whisk all the ingredients except the ghee together in a large bowl until smooth. Transfer to an airtight container and leave on the work surface at room temperature for 24 hours.

The next day, whisk the batter to a thick (double/heavy) cream consistency.

Heat the ghee in a frying pan. Tip the ghee out and set aside. Add 100 ml (3½ fl oz) of the pancake batter to the pan and, working quickly, swirl the pan so an even thin layer covers the base and sides of the pan. Add a little of the reserved ghee to the top of the pancake and lots of black pepper to the wet side of the pancake along with salt to taste. Flip onto the other side and cook briefly, 3 minutes total cooking time, then remove the pancake from the pan. Repeat to make three more pancakes. Keep warm.

Preheat the oven to 220°C (430°F) with the grill setting turned on, or use a salamander grill.

Combine all the ingredients for the spice mix in a bowl.

For the bone marrow, using a large kitchen knife, cut each vertebra on the spine to separate each piece of bone marrow, then rub the marrow with the spice mix. Stand the marrow pipes up on a baking tray and cook for 6 minutes until coloured and any flesh on the bone is cooked.

Sprinkle with some more salt and serve with the warmed harissa and pancakes.

See photo on page 219.

Sweet & Sour Albacore, Radicchio & Hazelnuts

This was one of the first dishes I put on the menu at Fish Face in Sydney as a young chef and I am still as proud of it now as I was twelve years ago. Yellowfin tuna, bonito or blue mackerel are all great alternate species.

SERVES: 6

600 g (1 lb 5 oz) trimmed centre-cut albacore loin
60 ml (2 fl oz/¼ cup) olive oil
1 head white radicchio, leaves torn into bite-sized pieces
sea salt flakes and freshly cracked black pepper
3 tablespoons roasted hazelnuts

Sweet & sour currant sauce

120 ml (4 fl oz) extra-virgin olive oil
150 g (5½ oz) French shallots, finely diced
150 ml (5 fl oz) white wine
375 ml (12½ fl oz/1½ cups) white-wine vinegar
150 ml (5 fl oz) water
75 g (2¾ oz/⅓ cup) caster (superfine) sugar
125 g (4½ oz/¾ cup) dried currants
sea salt flakes and freshly cracked black pepper

Preheat the oven to the lowest possible temperature.

For the sweet and sour sauce, heat the oil in a saucepan and sweat the shallots over a low heat for 15 minutes until just golden. Add the wine, vinegar, water, sugar, currants and a little salt and pepper and simmer briskly for 4 minutes until the shallots are very tender and the sauce is thick and syrupy. You should have 225 ml (7½ fl oz) of sauce after the reduction. Cool and chill until needed.

Cut the albacore loin into even-sized quarter planks, then chill, uncovered, in the refrigerator.

Place a wire rack inside a baking tray to act as a trivet to cook the albacore on.

Cut some baking paper to fit the size of the wire rack and, using a small knife, cut enough holes over the paper to allow the juices to strain through during cooking. Arrange the fish on the prepared wire rack and place in the oven. The oven should be between 90–100°C (194–212°F) throughout the cooking process. If you feel the oven is hotter than this then rest a pair of tongs or a wooden spoon in the door to hold the oven ajar. The internal temperature for the fish should be 40°C (104°F) when measured with a probe thermometer. Ideally, the fish should still look quite raw but with a gently cooked texture (be careful here as, unfortunately, albacore dries out very quickly during cooking).

Meanwhile, heat the olive oil in a frying pan over a high heat and sauté the radicchio leaves. Season well with salt and, at the last minute when the leaves are blistered and lightly wilted, add the roast hazelnuts and 4 generous tablespoons of the sweet and sour sauce. Keep warm.

Leave the albacore to rest briefly, then slice three slices per portion. Brush with olive oil, season with sea salt, cracked black pepper and drape over the sweet and sour radicchio and hazelnuts. Serve.

ALTERNATIVE FISH:
Bonito
Mackerel
Tuna

Fish Sausage Roll

The public school I attended in East Maitland had a memorable sausage roll, and one that I can remember had just the right amount of seasoning, fat and crispness from the pastry. I'm not 100 per cent sure of what was in it, but I wanted to try to replicate it by producing this version with fish. In the restaurant we serve this with a tomato sauce made from native bush tomato, but it's delicious with anything.

MAKES 8

4 square sheets puff pastry
plain (all-purpose) flour, for dusting

Filling

375 g (13 oz) ocean trout or sea
    trout belly
75 g (2¾ oz) fresh scallop meat
500 g (1 lb 2 oz oz) white fish, such
    as bream, flathead or whiting
1 onion, grated on a box grater
1 tablespoon salt
1¾ teaspoons ground white pepper
1¾ teaspoons ground fennel seeds
freshly grated nutmeg, to taste
15 g (½ oz/½ cup) chopped flat-leaf
    (Italian) parsley

Egg wash

2 whole eggs
1 egg yolk
1 tablespoon white sesame seeds
sea salt flakes

Before starting, chill all the parts of a food processor capable of blending fish to a puree. Have a bowl of ice ready. Once the food processor is chilled, blend the trout, scallop meat and white fish separately into smooth pastes. Combine the fish purees together and season with all the remaining ingredients. Keep this fish puree chilled over the bowl of ice.

Mix all the egg wash ingredients together in a bowl. Arrange the puff pastry sheets on a lightly floured work surface and arrange large spoonfuls of the fish mix on the pastry in the shape of a log. Using egg wash, brush the surrounding pastry liberally, then roll into the shape of a sausage roll. Either fold up the ends of the pastry to seal or cut to expose the ends. Brush the sausage roll with egg wash and chill for 30 minutes until set.

Meanwhile, preheat the oven to 200°C (400°F). Brush the sausage roll with more egg wash, then season with sea salt and bake for 15 minutes, or until the pastry is golden and the filling, when checked with a skewer, is hot to the touch. Serve with a generous spoonful of ketchup.

ALTERNATIVE FISH:
Arctic char
Hake
Salmon

Pot-roasted Rock Flathead & its Roe, Black Garlic & Pepper

This is a dish inspired by my time at Fish Face in Sydney. John dory, mirror dory or Murray cod are all fantastic alternatives to use in place of flathead for this recipe, but there is something about this rock flathead that I couldn't get past. The skin is sticky, the roe is sweet and the flesh stands up to the robust caramel flavours of the black garlic.

SERVES 2

2 x 300 g (10½ oz) rock flathead, bone in
100 g (3½ oz) butter, coarsely chopped
2 teaspoons coarsely crushed black peppercorns
8 black garlic cloves
2 tablespoons scraped flathead roe
200 ml (7 fl oz) Brown Fish Stock (ideally rock flathead, see page 67)
lemon juice, to taste
sea salt flakes
250 g (9 oz/5 cups) English spinach leaves

For the flathead, the pin bones can be removed without filleting the whole fish by opening the belly cavity and making an incision down both sides of the spine on the top half of the fish closest to the head. Pull out all of the fine bones using tweezers.

Preheat the oven to 200°C (400°F).

Melt the butter with the peppercorns in a large cast-iron frying pan over a medium heat until just beginning to foam. Add the fish and coat the skin all over with the pepper butter. Don't colour the skin. Add the black garlic and flathead roe. Turn the fish so the belly cavity is on the bottom of the pan. Add the stock and bring to the boil. Cover with aluminium foil, then roast in the oven for 4 minutes.

Turn the fish belly side up and return to the oven for a further 4 minutes, then remove from the oven, turn the fish the right way up and leave to rest on a plate.

Return the pan to a medium heat on the stove and cook until the juices are reduced, very thick and shiny. Season with lemon juice and a little salt, if required. Add the spinach and wilt for 30 seconds. To serve, spoon the spinach under the cooked fish and spoon the thick garlic and roe sauce over the fish to glaze. Serve.

ALTERNATIVE FISH:
John dory
Gurnard
Turbot

Fish Wellington

A Wellington, at least in my family, has been seen to be something of extravagance and only cooked on special occasions. The idea to produce a fish Wellington is in line with the traditional thinking behind a coulibiac, a traditional Russian fish pie. This is another fish dish that presents itself extremely well at the table, showing a great deal of technique and flair but also a lot of love and generosity.

SERVES 6

1 whole ocean or sea trout fillet, skinned and pin-boned
4 nori sheets
500 g (1 lb 2 oz) ready-made puff pastry
plain (all-purpose) flour, for dusting

Mushroom & lentil puree

150 g (5½ oz) ghee
1 kg (2 lb 3 oz oz) field mushrooms, coarsely chopped
100 g (3½ oz) butter, coarsely chopped
1 onion, finely chopped
6 garlic cloves, finely chopped
½ tablespoon finely chopped thyme
sea salt flakes
125 g (4½ oz/¾ cup) cooked black lentils, strained

Egg wash

2 whole eggs
1 egg yolk
1 tablespoon white sesame seeds
sea salt flakes

For the mushrooms, heat 75 g (2¾ oz) ghee in a large pot over a medium heat and cook the mushrooms in two batches until golden, about 10–12 minutes each batch. Add all the fried mushrooms back to the pot, then turn the heat up high. Add the butter, onion, garlic and thyme and sauté for 10 minutes until tender and the mushrooms have little to no moisture left. Season with salt to taste, then pulse in a food processor until finely chopped. Drain any excess fat or moisture from the mushroom mix, add the lentils and stir to combine. Cool.

To assemble, cut the trout fillet in half widthways, then pick the tail half up and position it on top of the other half, ensuring the loin side sits in line with the belly side, so it creates a seamless appearance.

Place a large square of plastic wrap on the work surface, then arrange the nori sheets on top so they overlap, forming a square. Spoon the mushroom and lentil puree onto the nori and spread it out. Position the fillet on top, then pick up the plastic wrap that is closest to you to bring the nori and mushroom puree up over the fillets, forming a log. The puree should completely enclose the fillet. Tie off the plastic wrap at both ends and chill overnight.

The next day, mix all the egg wash ingredients together in a bowl. Roll out a large square of the very chilled pastry that exceeds both the width and height of the trout log on a lightly floured work surface.

Cut the plastic wrap from the outside of the trout and position the fish in the centre of the pastry. Brush all corners of the pastry with egg wash and roll up over the trout log. Trim off any excess pastry and brush with more egg wash. Chill for at least 1 hour.

Preheat the oven to 220°C (430°F). Brush more egg wash over the Wellington and season lightly with sea salt. Bake for 20–25 minutes until brown and the interior temperature has reached 48°C (118°F) on a probe thermometer.

Leave to rest for 10 minutes, then carve the Wellington into six even slices and serve with good crunchy salad leaves.

ALTERNATIVE FISH:
Coral trout
Rainbow trout
Salmon

Glazed Cobia Christmas Ham

This is one of the most exciting dishes that I have created. The first year we opened Saint Peter I thought, 'How good would it be to try and firstly, achieve the look of a glazed Christmas leg ham on a fish and secondly, make it delicious?' The first version of the ham ticked the aesthetic box although I had issues with the thick skin I had chosen and when it came to taste, it was as smoky as I'd hoped but lacked the seasoning that is so desirable in a Christmas ham. The following year we tried again, but this time with greater success among a number of varying species.

SERVES 10–12

1 x approx. 4 kg (8 lb 13 oz) cobia tail or best alternative, such as swordfish or coral trout
24 cloves
100 g (3½ oz) hickory or cherry wood chips

Cure (120 g/4 oz cure per 1 kg/2 lb 3 oz fish)

40 g (1½ oz) caster (superfine) sugar
80 g (2¾ oz/¼ cup) fine salt
1 teaspoon ground cloves
15 g (½ oz) thyme leaves
¼ teaspoon nitrate
1 tablespoon toasted cracked black pepper
1 fresh bay leaf, finely chopped

Glaze spice mix

100 g (3½ oz) ground cinnamon
½ teaspoon ground clove
½ teaspoon ground star anise
1 teaspoon ground all spice

Glaze

180 g (6½ oz/½ cup) honey
360 ml (12 fl oz) red-wine vinegar
1 tablespoon glaze spice mix (see above)
1 tablespoon dijon mustard

For this particular recipe, we recommend you use the lower half of the fish. Request that the fish be cut just below the fish's anus so the flesh that remains on the bone is free of pin bones. The other half of the fish can be cured as well as a separate piece.

Determine how big the fish is that you are curing and work out how much cure you will need to make. Combine all the curing mix ingredients in a clean bowl. Wearing disposable gloves, rub the cobia tail with the mix until covered. Place on a stainless-steel tray or in a plastic container lined with baking paper. Cover with baking paper and leave to cure in the refrigerator for 5 days, turning the cobia every day. Wear disposable gloves each time to avoid contaminating.

Once the cobia is cured, remove from the tray, rinse the cure from the fish and pat dry with paper towel. Score the skin with a sharp blade to resemble the pattern of a Christmas ham, then add a clove where the cuts crossover.

To smoke this ham, an oven can be used, set to the lowest temperature. Make sure the kitchen is well ventilated. Place a saucepan full of soaked smoking chips in the bottom. Light the chips and allow the smoke to flood the oven. Smoke the fish for 2 hours, or until the internal temperature of the fish reaches 40°C (104°F) when measured with a probe thermometer. Leave to rest, then chill overnight.

For the glaze spice mix, combine all the ingredients and store in an airtight container until needed.

To make the glaze, bring all the ingredients to the boil in a saucepan over a medium–high heat and cook for 30 minutes, or until reduced by half (be sure to avoid over-reducing as the honey can often become too bitter). Set aside at room temperature.

Preheat the oven to 200°C (400°F).

Brush the fish with the glaze to cover the outside, then arrange on a wire rack set inside a large stainless-steel tray and cook for 20 minutes. Remove from the oven and brush with the glaze. At this point the skin will be both softening and taking colour. Cook for a further 15 minutes, or until the skin is completely glazed and the skin is tender and has crisp edges. The fish will have warmed through to the bone and can be carved and served.

Serve with your favourite Christmas salads, sauces and vegetables.

ALTERNATIVE FISH:
John dory
Mahi-mahi
Wild kingfish

See photo on following pages.

Roetato Bake

This recipe to me is more of an accompaniment to a main course, and makes a fantastic vehicle for a number of different fish eggs, sour cream and chives.

SERVES 4

4 medium waxy potatoes, such as desiree, cut into 2–3 mm (¹⁄₁₆–⅛ in) thick slices
240 g (8½ oz) ghee, melted and warmed
400 g (14 oz) scraped fish roe from mirror dory or john dory
2 tablespoons marjoram leaves
sea salt flakes and freshly cracked black pepper
3 large banana shallots, finely diced
150 g (5 oz) sour cream
2 bunches chives, finely chopped
100 g (3½ oz) sea urchin tongues, cleaned
100 g (3½ oz) salmon roe

Preheat the oven to 200°C (400°F).

Add the potato slices to a large bowl with the warm melted ghee and mix until the potatoes are coated. Add the roe, marjoram and season with salt, then mix until the potatoes are coated.

Layer the potatoes in four one-egg size pans or use a large muffin tin, fanning around the base of the pan, then repeating in the opposite direction as you build. When the pans are full add another two layers on top as the potato will decrease in size during cooking. Place baking paper on top and bake for 25–30 minutes until the potatoes are tender.

Leave the potatoes to stand for at least 10 minutes to allow the residual heat to finish cooking them, then tip them from the pan onto a warmed serving plate. While the potato is still warm, place a spoonful of diced shallot in the centre followed by a generous spoonful of sour cream. Add a spoonful of cut chives to the top and a twist of black pepper and sea salt. Add 3–4 sea urchin tongues and a spoonful of salmon roe around the sour cream to serve.

ALTERNATIVE FISH:
Hake
Lumpfish
Turbot

Hot Smoked Fish Turducken

The butterflying of these fish is a job for your fish shop to undertake but, really, the deboning of the fish is the only fiddly part of this recipe. This dish is definitely a show stopper – try serving at your next special occasion.

SERVES 12

2 kg (4 lb 6 oz) boneless, butterflied ocean trout or sea trout, head and tail on
1 kg (2 lb 3 oz) boneless, butterflied Murray cod
1 kg (2 lb 3 oz) yellowfin tuna loin, trimmed
100 g (3½ oz) soaked iron bark or other hardwood wood chips

Brine

400 g (14 oz/1⅓ cups) fine salt
8 litres (270 fl oz/32 cups) cold water

For the brine, combine the salt and water together and stir until the salt has dissolved. Place the fish in separate bowls and pour over the brine. Leave to stand overnight.

The next day, thoroughly dry the fish with paper towel. Lay the trout out in front of you with the tail closest to you. Place the Murray cod on top of the trout in the same position, the tail end closest to you, then place the tuna in the centre of the Murray cod. Using kitchen twine, truss the fish together ensuring that each fish remains in position and the bellies of the fish join up creating a seamless finish.

To smoke the fish, an oven can be used set to the lowest temperature. Make sure the kitchen is well ventilated. Place a saucepan full of soaked smoking chips in the bottom. Light the chips and allow the smoke to flood the oven. Smoke the fish for 2 hours, or until the internal temperature of the fish reaches 40°C (104°F) when tested with a probe thermometer. Leave to rest, then chill overnight.

Serve chilled or brushed with a little oil, season with sea salt and return to an oven preheated to 240°C (475°F) to crisp the skin for 10 minutes. Rest, then carve and serve hot.

ALTERNATIVE FISH:
Hake
Rainbow trout
Salmon

See photo on following pages.

Fish Part-y Pie

With these little pies I have tried to translate the deliciousness and almost nostalgic feeling of eating a party pie as a kid into a waste-minimising vehicle to show the full potential of a fish.

SERVES 4

Sauce

50 g (1¾ oz) butter
50 g (1¾ oz/⅓ cup) plain (all-purpose) flour
550 ml (17 fl oz/2 cups) hot Brown Fish Stock (ideally john dory, see page 67)
sea salt flakes and freshly cracked black pepper
1 john dory roe sack, scraped, approx. 100 g (3½ oz)
200 g (7 oz) john dory fillet, skinless and cut into 3 cm (1¼ in) chunks
2 sheets puff pastry
oil spray
plain (all-purpose) flour, for dusting

Filling

60 g (2 oz) ghee
80 g (2¾ oz) john dory liver
1 leek, chopped
1 tablespoon finely chopped tarragon
1 small smoked fish heart (see page 74), grated on a microplane (optional)
1 small smoked fish spleen (see page 74), grated on a microplane (optional)

Egg wash

2 whole eggs
1 egg yolk

For the sauce, melt the butter in a heavy-based saucepan over a medium heat. Add the flour and stir for 5 minutes, or until a roux forms. Gradually add the stock in three parts, combining well after each addition and being sure to remove any lumps. Add a little more stock if it's too thick. Once all the liquid is added, season and cook for a further 8–10 minutes. Whisk in the roe so the eggs separate through the sauce. Remove from the heat, add the john dory chunks and cover with baking paper to prevent a skin forming.

For the filling, heat the ghee in a frying pan over a high heat and cook the liver for 1 minute until caramelised on both sides. Drain on paper towel.

In the same pan at the same temperature with the same ghee, sauté the leek for 5–6 minutes until tender. Season with a little salt, then drain with the liver. Cut the liver into 3 x 3 cm (1¼ x 1¼ in) chunks and add to the john dory sauce. Add the cooked leeks, seasoning, tarragon and smoked grated offal, if using, then chill in the refrigerator.

Mix the egg wash ingredients together. To prepare the pie tins, use a standard muffin tin with a 7.5 cm (3 in) diameter and spray lightly with spray oil to make sure the pastry doesn't stick during cooking. Spread the pastry out on a lightly floured work surface and, using a 12 cm (4¾ in) diameter ring cutter, cut four discs of pastry from one sheet of pastry. Fit each disc into the base of the tin.

Using an 8 cm (3¼ in) ring cutter, cut out four rings of pastry for the lids from the other sheet of pastry. Add 2 tablespoons of the filling to each pie base, then brush the edge of the base pastry with egg wash. Brush the pastry lids with egg wash on one side too, then place this, egg wash side down, on top of the filling to cover. Using your fingers, crimp to enclose the filling, or use a fork to seal the edges. Brush the tops with more egg wash and chill for at least 30 minutes.

Preheat the oven to 200°C (400°F). Brush the pies with more egg wash and bake for 12–15 minutes until the pastry is a deep golden brown and the filling is hot.

Serve the pies hot with your favourite condiment (I always like mustard or tomato chutney).

ALTERNATIVE FISH:
Coral trout
Hake
Pearl perch

See photo on previous page.

Vanilla Cheesecake, John Dory Roe Biscuit, Raspberries & Lime

Outside of the lemon tart, whenever I think of desserts that could go on the menu at Saint Peter I think first of how I could possibly utilise a part of a fish. Not for the shock value of it but ultimately because I see delicious possibilities. One of these possibilities was realised when producing this cheesecake recipe, through the addition of fish roe to a conventional biscuit crumb to give it both additional seasoning and texture. The resulting biscuit is lightly salty and has a savouriness to it which is both unexplainable but also delicious. This biscuit is now the catalyst for further thoughts around using fish in desserts.

SERVES 6

Cheesecake

6 g (¼ oz) leaf gelatine
165 ml (2¼ fl oz) pouring cream (single/light)
115 g (4 oz/½ cup) cream cheese
50 g (1¾ oz/¼ cup) caster (superfine) sugar
2 whole vanilla beans, split in half and seeds scraped out
½ teaspoon vanilla extract
165 ml (5½ fl oz) thick (double/heavy) cream
110 g (4 oz) sour cream

John dory roe biscuit

100 g (3½ oz/⅔ cup) plain (all-purpose) flour
150 g (5½ oz/1½ cups) almond meal (ground almonds)
100 g (3½ oz/½ cup) caster (superfine) sugar
50 g (1¾ oz) honey
100 g (3½ oz/½ cup) unsalted butter
100 g (3½ oz) fresh john dory roe

To decorate

600 g (1 lb 5 oz/4¾ cups) raspberries
2 tablespoons fructose
50 ml (1¾ fl oz) verjuice
6 tablespoons john dory roe biscuit (see above)
½ teaspoon sea salt flakes
2 tablespoons extra virgin olive oil
juice of 1 lime

For the cheesecake, line a 500 ml (17 fl oz/2 cup) terrine mould with baking paper. Soften the gelatine in ice-cold water for 5 minutes. Gently warm 65 ml (2¼ fl oz) of the pouring cream in a small pan until it reaches 60–65°C (140–149°F). Remove from the heat, squeeze the softened gelatine and add to the warm cream. Mix until the gelatine has dissolved. Leave in a warm place.

Beat the cream cheese in a stand mixer fitted with a paddle attachment for 5 minutes, or until softened. Combine the caster sugar and vanilla seeds, then add this to the cream cheese, along with the cream and gelatine mixture, vanilla extract and the remaining 100 ml (3½ fl oz) pouring cream and mix until combined and silky smooth.

Whip the 165 ml (5½ fl oz) thick cream and sour cream together until soft peaks form, then fold into the cheesecake mix. Pour into the prepared mould and chill for at least 3 hours, or overnight.

Meanwhile, for the biscuits, preheat the oven to 150°C (300°F/Gas 2). Combine all the ingredients in a stand mixer fitted with a paddle attachment and mix to a soft breadcrumb-like consistency. Roll this loose dough between two sheets of baking paper, place on a baking sheet and bake for 20 minutes, or until golden brown. Leave to cool, then break the biscuits into a crumble. Set aside.

For the decoration, add 300 g (10½ oz/2½ cups) of the raspberries to a heatproof bowl along with the fructose and verjuice, cover with plastic wrap and set over a saucepan of gently simmering water. Leave for 15 minutes until the berries are soft. Strain and set the fruit aside for another use, then chill the juice until needed.

To serve, slice the cheesecake with a hot knife and place on serving plates. Add the remaining raspberries to a bowl and dress with a little of the chilled juice. Spoon the raspberries and 1–2 tablespoons of the chilled juice onto each plate, followed by a generous tablespoon of the roe biscuit, a pinch of sea salt, 1 teaspoon olive oil and a squeeze of lime juice.

See photo on following page.

Fish Fat Chocolate Caramel Slice

We cooked this dish for an OzHarvest dinner with Massimo Bottura in 2017 to show that a delicious dessert could be produced from the discarded items of a fish. The recipe was developed by myself, my wife, Julie Niland, and Alanna Sapwell, who was a chef at Saint Peter. It required a great deal of thought and consideration to produce something ultimately delicious but also worthy of being a dessert good enough for one of the best chefs in the world.

SERVES 16

Chocolate base

190 g (6½ oz) butter, softened
215 g (7½ oz) caster (superfine) sugar
1 tablespoon cocoa powder
105 g (3½ oz) egg yolks
75 g (2¾ oz) whole eggs
225 g (8 oz) dark chocolate (at least 70% cocoa solids), melted
340 g (12 oz) egg whites

Chocolate custard

235 g (8½ oz) unsalted butter
345 g (12 oz) dark chocolate (at least 70% cocoa solids), broken into pieces
6 eggs
210 g (7½ oz) caster (superfine) sugar

For the chocolate base, preheat the oven to 170°C (340°F). Line two 30 x 20 cm (12 x 8 in) baking trays with baking paper.

Beat the butter, 90 g (3 oz/⅓ cup) of the caster sugar and the cocoa in a stand mixer fitted with a paddle attachment until pale and the sugar has dissolved. Gradually add the egg yolks and eggs on medium speed in three batches, making sure they are incorporated after each addition. Stop the mixer and add the melted chocolate. Turn the mixer back on gradually to a medium speed until the chocolate is incorporated.

In a separate bowl, whisk the egg whites with the remaining 125 g (4½ oz/½ cup) caster sugar for 4 minutes, or until stiff peaks form, then gently fold through the chocolate base until incorporated. Spread the mixture over the prepared baking trays and bake for 20 minutes, or until the cake is just set and a skewer inserted in the centre comes out clean. Chill for 1 hour.

For the custard, preheat the oven to 170°C (340°F). Line a 30 x 20 cm (12 x 8 in) baking tray with baking paper.

Melt the butter and chocolate together in a heatproof bowl set over a saucepan of near-simmering water. Make sure the bottom of the bowl doesn't touch the water. When melted, mix well to combine.

Whisk the eggs and sugar together in a stand mixer until the sugar has dissolved. Fold the chocolate into the egg mix, then pour into the prepared baking tray. Place the baking tray in a larger baking tray or roasting tin, then pour in enough hot water to go halfway up the smaller baking tray. Cover the larger tray with aluminium foil, making sure it is sealed, and bake for 40 minutes, or until the custard is just set.

Remove from the oven, uncover and, if the custard isn't set, then leave it in the warm water. Cool overnight in the refrigerator until chilled.

See photo on previous page.

Chocolate glaze

8 titanium-grade gelatine leaves
500 ml (17 fl oz/2 cups) ice-cold
    water
140 ml (4½ fl oz) water
180 g (6½ oz/¾ cup) caster (superfine)
    sugar
120 g (4½ oz/½ cup) pouring (single/
    light) cream
60 g (2 oz/½ cup) good-quality high
    percentage cocoa powder
100 g (3½ oz) Valrhona neutral glaze
    (can buy online)

Fish fat salted caramel

125 g (4½ oz) fish fat (cobia or Murray
    cod)
500 g (1 lb 2 oz) caster (superfine)
    sugar
250 g (9 oz/1 cup) thick (double/
    heavy) cream
2 vanilla beans, split open lengthways
    and seeds scraped out
75 g (2¾ oz) liquid glucose
200 g (7 oz) butter
½ teaspoon sea salt flakes

To assemble

4 glazed chocolate cakes
4 strips Fish fat salted caramel
    (see above)
1 tablespoon toasted fennel seeds
2 tablespoons caramelised fish scales
    (see page 69)
sea salt flakes
120 g (4½ oz/½ cup) sour cream

To assemble the cake, lay the cake base on a chopping board, place the set custard tray upside down on top and tip the custard out onto the cake. Firmly push down to stick them together. Peel the baking paper off the custard and, using a very hot sharp knife, cut the cake into bars, about 10 cm (4 in) long and 4–5 cm (1½–2 in) wide. Arrange the bars on a wire rack set over a tray and chill for 1 hour.

Meanwhile, make the glaze. Soften the gelatine in the ice-cold water for 15 minutes. Bring the water, sugar and cream to the boil in a saucepan, then add the cocoa and mix well.

Melt the neutral glaze in a separate small pan over a low heat. Add the neutral glaze to the wet mix and bring to the boil for 5 minutes. Remove from the heat and add the softened gelatine. Combine and set aside in a warm place, if not using immediately. The glaze needs to be warmed to 35°C (95°F).

Pour the warm glaze over the bars, then chill for 1 hour on the wire rack until set. Once set, trim off any glaze that has stuck to the base and chill in an airtight container until required.

For the caramel, line two 30 x 20 cm (12 x 8 in) baking trays with baking paper.

Melt the fat in a saucepan over a low heat for 10–12 minutes, or until liquid. Keep warm.

Combine 250 g (9 oz) of the sugar, the cream, vanilla bean (pod) and seeds together in a saucepan and warm over a low heat for 5 minutes, or until the sugar has dissolved. Cool.

Mix the remaining 250 g (9 oz) caster sugar and the liquid glucose together in a large heavy-based pot and cook over a medium–high heat for 10 minutes, without stirring, until the sugar has dissolved. Cook until the caramel has reached the desired colour, then add the vanilla cream in three batches, being careful as it will spit, and boil rapidly. Cook until it reaches a temperature of 128°C (262°F), then remove from the heat and, using a whisk, whisk in the butter, fat and salt. Pour the caramel across the prepared baking trays in a thin layer, about 5 mm (¼ in) thick and cool completely at room temperature for 2 hours. Chill overnight until set.

The next day, tip the caramel onto a chopping board and, using a very hot, sharp knife, cut the caramel into 10 x 2 cm (4 x ¾ in) lengths. Chill in an airtight container until required.

To assemble, place the four glazed chocolate bars down in front of you. Arrange the caramel lengths in the centre of each chocolate bar, then season with 6–7 fennel seeds, add 6–7 caramelised fish scales and a few salt flakes. Place the sour cream into a piping (icing) bag fitted with a fluted piping nozzle and pipe the sour cream down both sides of the caramel. There should be a gap of 2 cm(¾ in) between the edge of the caramel and the edge of the chocolate. Serve at room temperature.

APPENDIX

A note to chefs on commercial dry-ageing

For chefs looking to invest in better fish storage and dry-ageing in a commercial environment it's important to establish meticulous sourcing and handling procedures for your fish supply, then consider investing in your cool room set-up.

The site where we opened Saint Peter had an existing conventional fan-powered cool room located behind the kitchen. Before opening we took a big risk in establishing a static chamber within this coolroom where we could hang large fish from rails and store smaller fish on custom designed drip trays. We didn't know if it would work and we hardly had the finances to pay for it. Our first social media posts showing our first fish (an 18 kg/40 lb mahi-mahi) hanging in our new fridge were met with some derision and scepticism – only fuelling our own doubt. Ultimately the gamble paid off and after much trial and error and adjustments by the fridge technicians we were able to start our experimentation with dry-ageing. The optimised storage conditions also allowed us to buy fish in bulk when it was at its best and cheapest.

The set-up at Saint Peter may be an ideal starting point for a small restaurant looking to store fish in more optimal conditions. We subdivided the coolroom, sacrificing about 25 per cent of the existing space to create a static interior chamber, which could be accessed by a door inside the main coolroom. The chamber was lined with copper coil that chilled the small space without use of a fan. This set-up allowed us to begin dry-ageing fish and storing fish in a static environment. Half the chamber was left empty except for a rail on the ceiling to allow large fish to hang from butcher's hooks. The other half was filled with custom-designed shelving to hold stainless-steel trays with drain plates for smaller fish and fillets.

When we opened Fish Butchery we decided to invest in a larger and more sophisticated set-up and installed cross fin coil technology in the ceiling of the cool room. In the opening weeks we experienced issues with the coils icing over, which stopped them working effectively and raised the temperature of the cool room, but after some tweaks the fridge was working well. An unexpected benefit of the cross fin technology compared to the copper coil set-up at Saint Peter is that it creates a lower humidity environment, which then acts to keep the skin dry without drying it out (as a fan would) while the fish ages. So since moving the storage and dry-ageing of Saint Peter's fish to Fish Butchery we have been able to achieve pan-fried fish with skin so crisp that it puffs away from the flesh like pork crackling.

Small fish, such as flathead, garfish and King George whiting would look fairly ridiculous hanging from butcher's hooks in your cool room. These fish are best stored in a single layer on a stainless-steel drain plate sitting inside a stainless-steel gastronome tray. These trays can be slotted into a hotel trolley. In a static fridge there is no need to cover the whole small fish. Fillets are best covered loosely with plastic freezer film.

Large fish are ideally stored hanging using butcher's hooks inserted through the fish's tail. This prevents the fish from sweating as it never comes into contact with a tray. Our coolroom was designed with rails that run parallel to the door opening so that fish hangs in 'curtains'. We have had to get creative with straps and ropes for very large fish, which the butcher's hooks cannot hold.

A note on my philosophy (and waste)

I don't understand how the 40–45 per cent (or, more to the point, the 55–60 per cent waste) that chefs are taught to expect a round fish to yield can be acceptable globally.

Saint Peter is a fish restaurant in Sydney, Australia that seats thirty-four people in one sitting. In a working week we will purchase in excess of 150 kg (331 lb) of fish, that's approx 25 kg (55 lb) fish a day. The average price for round fish in Sydney including the premium fish we buy is $20/kg. If we were to apply the industry standard yield expectations of 40–45 per cent then, at $500 a day, that's a total loss of $300 and a yield of $200. Now I understand that bones are used for stock and some restaurants will be grilling the fish's collar meat over charcoal but this only represents a small percentage of the 'loss'.

For example, a 17 kg (38 lb) line-caught bar cod I bought whole at $24/kg cost me $408. Based on a 44 per cent yield, this represents a cost of $179 of 'usuable' fillet. The other 56 per cent loss is seen as a cost of $228. The usable fillet weighs 7.45 kg (16 lb) and will yield 26 x 200 g (7 oz) portions that, to the eye, are desirable and worthy of their place on an a la carte menu. Each portion costs $15.69 and would need to be sold at a minimum of $60 in a restaurant to represent a 'profitable' margin once overheads are factored in. To consider that if the efforts of this book only helped you gain a further 10 per cent of the 'loss'

you would have an extra 1.73 kg (4 lb) from that bar cod ($41.50) to play with.

In a small business this represents a huge opportunity to play your part for a more sustainable future, but also an opportunity to use more of what you are paying a premium for. It can be difficult to determine whether the additional labour it takes to dissect the fish into every single part and make it delicious is 'worth it' from a financial point of view. One thing we have always found at Saint Peter is that when food costs go down, wage costs go up (and vice versa).

It is in recent years that I have focused all my energy into these 'secondary' items. I was fortunate to be in a kitchen throughout my training that sourced a lot of whole fish every day of the week, so seeing the organs of the fish was part of a daily routine of scaling and gutting. There came a point though that I started weighing the offal that was removed from the fish and noticed some startling numbers. Some livers from john dory were equal to the weight of the fillet itself and roe from a mahi-mahi made up 12 per cent of the body weight. Not only was I looking at this as a product that had an actual dollar value, I saw so much potential in this offal to produce recipes from. I started with the obvious – salting roe to produce what was a primitive style of bottarga, before progressing to pan-frying fish liver simply with parsley on good sourdough toast (now a staple and favourite on the Saint Peter menu).

INDEX

ACKNOWLEDGEMENTS

I feel writing a book, in any field, is quite a privilege and carries a weight of responsibility – a responsibility that consumes your thoughts.

I am very lucky to be surrounded by some extraordinary people in my life. None more so than my beautiful wife, Julie. Julie's love, patience and care for everything she does is superhuman – she is one of the most hardworking and inspiring people I know. How she manages to run two businesses with me and be the mother of our three beautiful children is completely beyond me. I am an extraordinarily lucky man.

To my family, Stephen, Marea, Elizabeth, Hayley and Ian, thank you for always being there every step of the way and supporting me. Without you all I really wouldn't have had the opportunity to write this book.

To my mentors, Peter Doyle, Stephen Hodges, Joe Pavlovich, Luke Mangan, Alex Woolley, and Elizabeth and Anthony Kocon. The words 'thank you' seem insignificant considering the extraordinary roles you have played in my career so far. You have all challenged me and pushed me to be better and I am forever grateful and privileged to have been one of your chefs.

To all the chefs past and present who have worked at Saint Peter and Fish Butchery: thank you all for your patience, hard work and dedication in a field that is so laborious and requires so much attention. A particular mention must go to the very talented opening team at Saint Peter who really brought it all to life – Wimmy Winkler, Alanna Sapwell, Oliver Penmit, Sean Conway and Camille Vangramberen – without all of you, Saint Peter would never have experienced the success that it has had. Finally, to Paul Farag and Todd Garratt for believing in Fish Butchery and working tirelessly to produce a totally unique brand. I am indebted to all of you.

I must also thank the extraordinary team at Hardie Grant for believing in such a unique book. To the talents of Jane Willson, Simon Davis, Daniel New, Rob Palmer, Steve Pearce, Jessica Brook and Kathy Steer. Thank you from the bottom of my heart for investing so much into this book and exceeding all of my expectations; it is amazing what can be achieved in a short space of time. Thanks also to the wonderful Monica Brown for your wisdom, constant support and belief.

Published in 2019 by Hardie Grant Books, an imprint of Hardie Grant Publishing

Hardie Grant Books (Melbourne)
Building 1, 658 Church Street
Richmond, Victoria 3121

Hardie Grant Books (London)
5th & 6th Floors
52–54 Southwark Street
London SE1 1UN

hardiegrantbooks.com

 A catalogue record for this book is available from the National Library of Australia

The Whole Fish Cookbook
ISBN 978 1 74379 553 8

10 9 8 7 6 5

Publishing Director: Jane Willson
Managing Editor: Marg Bowman
Project Editor/Editor: Simon Davis
Copy Editor: Kathy Steer
Design Manager: Jessica Lowe
Designer: Daniel New
Photographer: Rob Palmer
Stylist: Steve Pearce
Styling Assistant: Jessica Brook
Props: Sage Creative Co, Batch Ceramics and AllFiredUp Pottery
Production Manager: Todd Rechner

Colour reproduction by Splitting Image Colour Studio
Printed in China by Leo Paper Products Ltd.

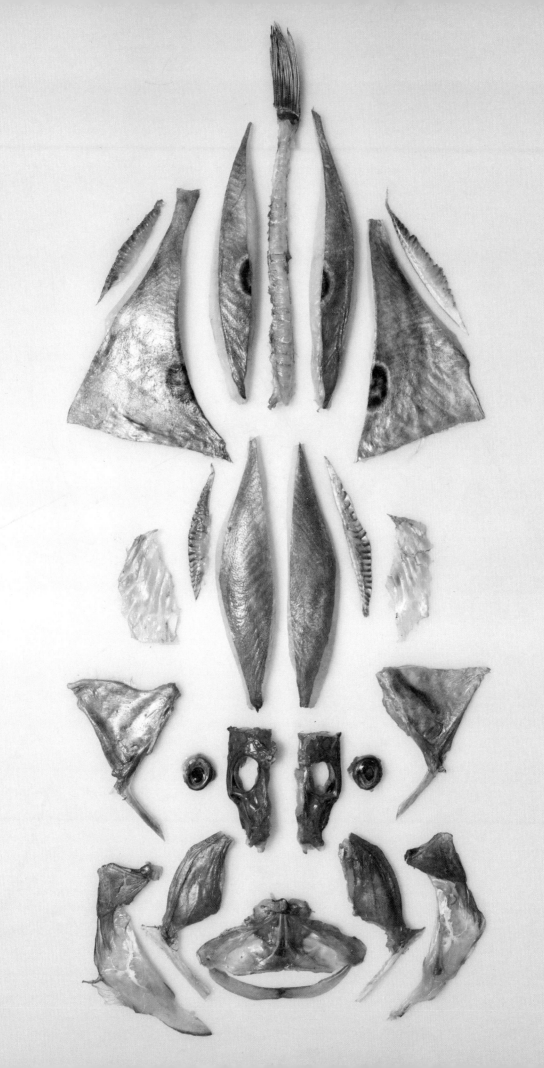

Equal parts comprehensive technical manual and a giant porthole into creativity, chef Niland's honest and pure approach to all things fish is inspiring. *The Whole Fish Cookbook* beautifully articulates the entire animal approach while methodically opening the reader's mind to how responsibility and innovation coexist.

GRANT ACHATZ

Here's one of those rare books that teaches you the basics. An inspiring read, and something to return to again and again — these pages are sure to be worn down quick.

RENÉ REDZEPI

If you love cooking fish, this book will be a revelation. You'll learn about dry-ageing to concentrate flavour, as well as using every part but the bubble from a fish's mouth!

RICK STEIN

I have followed Josh for such a long time and adore him and his use of every part of a fish – what a trailblazer he is ... this book is for home cooks as much as chefs and I applaud it.

MAGGIE BEER

There's no other chef in the world that I would rather have scale me with his knife, dry-age me, roast me, glaze me, rest me, slice me, serve me than this powerful spirit! Thank you Josh for paying attention and caring the way you do! You are a shining light!

MATTY MATHESON

Josh Niland's uncompromising discipline combined with his unique scale-to-tail, sustainable seafood philosophy has led to a revolution in the way we think, feel, prepare and eat seafood.

KYLIE KWONG